Who Will it Hurt When I Die?

Dennis Hall

Who Will it Hurt When I Die?

First published in 2013 by

Yellowtail Publishing Limited
4 Lombard Street
London
EC3V 9HD

Email publish@yellowtail.co.uk

ISBN 978-1-910011-00-3

Cover illustration by Meredith Owen
Design and Layout Charlotte Mouncey
www.bookstyle.co.uk

Dedicated to my Mother, Christine Hall.
If only I knew then what I know now.

Acknowledgements

AT FIRST, THE process of writing a book appears a solitary task. In reality there are numerous people who help shape and influence the finished product, or who isolate the writer from day to day distractions that would otherwise get in the way.

So much of this book relies on other people's experiences, and I want to acknowledge all those who were kind enough to spare me the time to share their stories, particularly the widows I spoke to. Not every story made it into the book, but each one helped shape my thinking. Thank you. Your willingness to share will hopefully make life easier for others.

I owe a huge debt of gratitude to my colleagues Mushtaq Jaigirdar and Phoebe Mayer. Mushtaq has been a constant force in our financial planning business, ensuring it keeps operating whilst I disappear to do more writing. I wouldn't have been able to achieve this book without his very able hand on the tiller. Thank you Mushtaq. Phoebe joined the team more recently, but quickly became a tremendous resource, and I've valued her input at every stage. She's a bright cookie and I'm glad she's on the team.

In November 2010 I was fortunate to meet Maria Nemeth - a very gifted person who has guided me through many difficulties with her mantra of focus, clarity, ease and grace. Through Maria I met Anita Gatehouse, a financial planner on a similar journey, and Anita has been a daily source of inspiration.

Thank you to all our clients, past and present. Your support provides the wherewithal for me to pursue projects like this.

Thanks also to my peers, who provide more support than I would ever admit to, or they could possibly imagine. Thanks to those who read some or all of the various drafts and particularly to Jon Cudby who took it upon himself to proof and edit - I am grateful. Thanks to Charlotte who brilliantly designed the layout of this book, despite receiving the manuscript in dribs and drabs. To my small army of reviewers including; Fi, Huda, Annie, and Kath - thank you.

A nod of recognition to the team at Entrevo who helped kick-start this journey, with special mention to Daniel and Andrew Priestley, whose words of advice I've quietly absorbed and turned into a plan. And to the KPI community; your encouragement means a lot.

Closer to home, gratitude for my family and friends who have put up with unanswered phone calls, and emails not returned, all without complaint. My mother has forgotten what I look like and probably thinks I've emigrated without telling her. And then there are my one year-old twin granddaughters, Anya and Orla, who I've visited twice only.

Bearing the brunt of my hermit-like existence has been my wife, Akiko. In this respect writing is a solitary task, and evening after evening, weekend after weekend, she has had to keep herself occupied. On writing days she provided nourishment at regular intervals, but otherwise allowed me to craft this book. Thanks Aki, I know I haven't said thank you enough.

Foreword

"I'M MORE THAN their financial adviser, I'm a confidante, and part of a trusted team providing lifelong peace of mind."

With these words, Dennis Hall sets a compassionate tone for one of the most informative books on financial planning that I have ever read. Dennis possesses a rare mix of sensitivity and technical expertise that will guide anyone who is willing to put his or her financial affairs in order, so that they and their families thrive. In this book, he turns his eye to the most difficult of subjects: the death of loved ones.

It's no secret that we are living in times of a great shift in the field of financial advice. At one time the financial adviser was sought primarily for his or her technical ability to design and implement investment portfolios. Now the field requires that same adviser to provide additional services of a more personal nature: helping clients design and attain the financial life goals that are most important and meaningful for them. This requires that the financial adviser have the capacity to work with people on their needs as well as their vision for the future.

This is easier said than done. First, many financial advisers have not been trained to have these sorts of conversations with clients. They have been taught how to analyze portfolios rather than helping clients to analyze how to attain cherished dreams.

Second, it is very difficult to talk with people about their relationship with money. I remember one coaching client who told me he would rather talk about anything else in his intimate personal life, than about how much money he made every month and how much he had in savings.

But talking about money is, in fact, intimate and personal. We are often taught that it is uncouth or improper to discuss such things. So we postpone the discussion. And, as Dennis so aptly illustrates in this book's stories, sometimes money is never talked about until it is, unfortunately, too late.

Dennis shows us what can happen when we don't have important financial conversations with those we love. His approach is deeply rigorous yet kind. We can begin to look for ourselves at what needs to be done so that no one need suffer needlessly when we pass away.

And this is the deeply satisfying aspect of this book. When we face and talk about money, when we plan for the inevitable future, we experience a sense of peace.

I have known Dennis, both as friend and colleague, for a number of years now. I have heard him speak about the necessity for financial advisers to develop the capacity to have intensive, yet respectful, conversations with clients about their desires and dreams for the future, and how their money lives can contribute to their vision.

In writing this book about leaving our loved ones with some sense of security in the face of unspeakable loss Dennis exhibits the traits of the new model for financial advisers. It is a book I will recommend my clients to read. It will make a difference in their lives, as it is already doing so in mine.

Maria Nemeth, PhD, MCC
Author of The Energy of Money.
Director of the Academy for Coaching Excellence
Sacramento, California. September, 2013

Contents

How this book is arranged

ONE THING BECAME clear at an early stage of this book's development; it had to be easy to pick up and even easier to read. If it was the slightest bit gloomy, technical, or depressing, it would fail to attract the kind of readers I was writing for.

Over the past few years I've had many conversations about death, its inevitability, and whether people's financial planning takes dying into account. Unsurprisingly, most people (with the exception of actuaries) told me death is too depressing to think about, and so they put it to the back of their mind. This reflects my twenty-five years' experience as a financial planner - people don't like talking about death or dying.

Death and money are perhaps the last taboo topics in our society, maybe because there's an intangible quality about them both. When we do get around to doing any financial planning, we generally focus on things occurring over short time frames, typically a few years at most. Even retirement is a difficult concept, particularly for younger people. That's partly the reason why our society is sleepwalking into a pension and retirement crisis. But that's another story.

So let's steel ourselves and look at death - I've consciously tried to write and design this book so that it is easy on the eye, and easy to read. Given the subject, I've found it a challenge. But hopefully I've succeeded, so that more people will have honest conversations about the financial consequences of death.

Being a realist I also know that a book focusing predominantly on financial planning will almost certainly remain on the shelf - unread. Therefore to make it easier to read I've arranged this book into two parts.

The first part is a collection of stories, anecdotes and real-life experiences. Most have been gathered from widows who told me about the financial difficulties they faced after their partner's death. Personally I've always found stories and anecdotes easier to relate to, especially if there is new information to absorb.

Real stories, however, rarely have fairytale endings, and many of the people who shared their experiences are still trying to find a 'new normal'. Some haven't achieved it yet, but have still been willing to share. And by sharing these real-life experiences they've shown us how easily things can go wrong. My job is to show you how, with some forward planning, each problem could have been avoided, or at least minimised.

(Because each story is real, involving real people, I have changed names, locations and any other identifying features to ensure their anonymity)

At intervals I'll ask you to stop and think about your own situation as it relates to the other person's story - are there any similarities? I'll also ask some questions to help you focus, and get clarity about where you are currently. Then you can decide if you need to do something to resolve the problem.

Having initially looked at various problems and how they arise, as well as ways to avoid them; the second part looks at the nuts and bolts of the individual 'solutions' that can used.

Part 2, therefore, provides more detail of things like Wills, life insurance, pensions and investment. It's not written as a technical guide, more a detailed glossary. There are better places to get information or advice should you want a deeper understanding of the legal and financial matters covered.

Toward the end of the book I've added a glossary of technical words or terms used in the book, though where possible I've tried to use everyday words instead of jargon.

Finally I've added a list of recommended books I've read and found particularly useful. I've included books covering bereavement, grief, and death; as well as those covering money, happiness and life. If the subject of bereavement and death leaves you breathless or worried there are some specific recommendations that may ease any anxiety you feel.

The biggest part of being a financial planner is helping people make good decisions regarding their money, so they can enjoy living life to the full. But asking the question "Who Will it Hurt When I Die?" acknowledges the potential for a surviving partner to experience financial difficulty, and this allows us to do something about it.

Introduction

IN 1992 MY father died. He was in his early fifties. One morning he left for work and he never came home. His death was sudden and unexpected, and left my mother emotionally and financially stricken.

I'd previously resigned from the Royal Marines for a career in financial services. I was the eldest of my siblings, so seniority and a smattering of financial knowledge meant I'd be the one helping my mother with her finances. I was woefully unprepared, and so was she.

For the first few weeks following my father's death everyone rallied round, and my mother did not have to cope alone. We were there for the funeral, the coroner's inquest, and the deluge of forms that accompany bereavement. But daily visits and phone calls soon fell away as everyone (including me) returned to their normal lives; everyone except my mother. Like so many recently bereaved widows she now faced an uncertain future.

I was no stranger to death. Whilst in the Marines I saw active service and witnessed people die. But until my father's death I hadn't seen how completely debilitating bereavement is - or how universal. I've since advised many widows, and seen how decision making can become impossible during bereavement.

In the weeks and months following bereavement people often avoid making financial decisions, or they end up making the wrong ones - each has a devastating effect on finances. The bereaved want the problems to go away, but instead are forced into making important decisions for which they're not adequately prepared. Of course, being ill-prepared is not for a lack of knowledge or intelligence, but rather that they're simply reacting to stress the only way the body knows how.

When stressed, the body releases chemicals designed to help us cope with danger. With long-term stress these chemicals accumulate and lead to an imbalance that severely impairs our decision making ability. Over time, stress can cause serious illness, and depression.

I've met too many widows who are financially insecure, and many others who simply made poor financial decisions. I asked myself "what could I do to prevent this happening", and the idea of writing a book was born. As part of my research I interviewed several widows to hear their stories. When I told them what I was doing they were genuinely open about their experiences, and generous with their time. But...

They told me I was barking up the wrong tree. In their experience a book for the recently bereaved would never work.

They said bereavement brought anxiety, fear and depression, to such an extent it took all their resources simply to survive. They hadn't deliberately set out to make things difficult for themselves, but at times during their bereavement they were unable to do anything. Reading a self-help book about finances? It wouldn't happen.

And though it makes a lot of sense now, it was an eye-opener when they told me.

It forced me to think again about what I was trying to do. Was I fixing the problem, or merely relieving the symptoms? Why was I expecting people to make important decisions at precisely the time they weren't able to?

If I was going to help I had to go to the heart of the problem. And the heart of the problem is this: people rarely think about what will happen when the unthinkable happens.

First of all, I had to encourage people to acknowledge the problem, and with sufficient time for them to do something about it. And then I had to provide the answers to the problems. It sounded simple enough but as I soon discovered, it was easier said than done. I burned a lot of midnight oil until I reached a stage where my early readers said it worked.

I noticed quite quickly that people preferred to read stories of other people's experiences, rather than facts and figures, or intellectual debates about death. The stories enabled them to share someone else's experiences before relating them to their own situation. Stories gently nudged them into thinking about the unthinkable; who really wants a lecture about financial planning? Telling stories is what good financial planners do.

For the past few years in my practice, I've been using what I've learned from researching and writing this book. For the couples I've been advising it's added a further dimension to the work we do together. We're not only developing financial strategies to support them during their lifetimes; we're providing a framework to support the survivor through bereavement and beyond.

I've also noticed that by helping people address these issues it enhances the client/adviser relationship, and I've become more than their financial adviser. I'm a confidante, and part of a trusted team providing lifelong peace of mind.

When looking through a long lens, even beyond their own lives, people's attitude toward their money changes. They look at money differently, use it differently, and generally look for ways to reduce complexity and to simplify finances.

This book shares the important things I have learned about helping people enjoy life at its best, whilst preparing for the worst.

COVER ILLUSTRATION: The Victorians used flowers to convey a variety of messages and emotions, the marigold was used to signify pain, sorrow and grief. The marigold is also used extensively in other cultures to symbolise death and remembrance. In pre-Hispanic Mexico for instance it was used as the flower of the dead, and it is still used in the "Day of the Dead" ceremonies.

Part One

Chapter One
One Man's Story

BEFORE STARTING I want to be clear about one thing; I'm not suggesting bereavement only affects widows. The death of anyone who is close hits hard, regardless of our gender or relationship to the deceased. Indeed, although the majority of my experience has been gained by working with widows, the following story shows how a mother's death deeply affected one man I was asked to help.

Meet George

Outwardly George was happy and content. A recently retired bachelor living in North London, he kept busy visiting friends and walking his neighbour's dogs. The latter providing some pocket money. What his neighbours didn't know was this 'pocket money' had been George's only income for several months.

They didn't know about the twelve months mortgage arrears, or the arrears on bank loans and unpaid overdrafts. Not even George was aware of his true predicament.

Until one day he received a knock at the door, and thinking it might be a neighbour he answered it. Standing in the doorframe was a bailiff. George was about to be evicted and the property repossessed. He fainted.

Stepping inside to help, the bailiff noticed a pile of unopened letters behind the front door, some turned out to be more than a year old. Among the most recent letters included those bearing the insignia of the Magistrates Court. These contained details of the eviction notice. And they remained unopened.

For more than a year George had not opened his mail. At some point things had become too much and he'd decided "out of sight, out of mind" was the best way of dealing with things. On the downside it meant he was unaware of his pending eviction.

Faced with an unusual situation the bailiff offered George a short lifeline. There would be no eviction that day, but he would return in one week's time. George was told to use the time to find alternative accommodation.

By now some neighbours had gathered round, and one offered to stay with George until he'd recovered from the shock. Over a cup of tea he told her about his mother's death, the unopened mail, and the eviction that would occur in a week's time.

She discovered George had been diagnosed with depression, and was taking prescription medicine. His mother had died a year earlier, leaving George the only surviving member of the family. With no one to share his grief, he found it difficult to cope, so he left his job and took early retirement.

But this didn't solve his problems, or make them go away. So he decided to avoid them and stopped opening his mail. He now passed the time walking his neighbour's dogs. This kept him out of the house and provided enough money to buy some food each day. He appeared cheerful enough to everyone, but behind the front door his problems were getting bigger. And then the bailiff arrived.

The following day one of the neighbours, a friend of mine, asked if I could do anything to help. It turned out George had several assets that would solve his immediate problems. We were able to clear his bank debts by cashing in a couple of long term savings policies.

Even though George had got himself onto the wrong side of his bank - a bank frequently voted among the best for customer satisfaction - I was surprised at how unhelpful they were, given the circumstances. As soon as they had received their money they closed his account. So on top of everything else, we then had to find a new bank - thankfully the Co-op Bank was prepared to open an account for George.

On the other hand, I was surprised at the efficiency and helpfulness of Norwich Union - now Aviva. They beat every deadline given to them as we raced against the clock to cash-in his policies. Perhaps we were lucky, but we found someone who took personal responsibility to help George get his money in time.

Having averted the immediate crisis we still had to look at how George would sustain himself in the future. Something was missing. I then discovered George hadn't yet claimed his retirement pension. There was a large tax-free lump sum, and more than a year's income that hadn't been paid. Things were looking up for George, and we were able to avoid the imminent eviction (with barely hours to spare).

If George had claimed his retirement benefits on time he would now be mortgage and debt free, and living a worry-free life. Sadly however, the additional penalties and costs raised his debts to a level where he couldn't repay them completely.

George kept his home, but still has a small mortgage. It takes a small slice of his pension, and will do for several years to come.

George's experience illustrates how bereavement can seriously affect someone's ability to cope, even if they appear to be functioning normally. He was unable to cope with the emotional demands he faced, and was only able to deal with things by ignoring his biggest problems. Denial and avoidance are not uncommon reactions during a period of bereavement. Sadly, none of his friends or neighbours knew he was in financial difficulty. It hadn't even crossed their minds.

Plan ahead to avoid a crisis

George's story also shows how an ordinarily financially literate person can make catastrophic financial errors following bereavement. Small problems will become big problems if they are not dealt with quickly.

Of course, we cannot anticipate every problem, but if we can plan for those we're aware of, it frees us to deal with any new problems that arise. In my experience whatever time is spent anticipating problems arising on death, is time well spent. It reduces the amount of stress and anxiety suffered by dependants and loved ones, and they are less likely to make costly financial mistakes.

No-one I've talked to wants to create unnecessary hardship for those they leave behind - and they all agreed it was sensible to plan ahead so as to reduce worry and stress.

However, that means having difficult conversations that you might prefer to avoid. I hope this book will encourage, and give you the resolve needed, to have those difficult and emotional conversations about what life would be like without you, or without your partner.

In my experience, when people start to have these conversations, they begin to discover the things that really matter to them - and it's not necessarily the things they've been striving for.

But before we go any further, I want to summarise the main lesson that I think this chapter shows us. In my introduction I identified a general avoidance or denial to even imagine, let alone plan for, death and the future of those left behind. George's story well illustrates how his self-denial (of his situation following his mother's death) had isolated him, and his issues, from those around him.

But if we are able to deal with our denial or our inability to ask for help, it provides a degree of mitigation or damage control – it would have helped George, and preserved his finances, thus providing greater security and peace of mind.

As the next chapter shows, it's easier to deal with these things before a crisis, rather than during a crisis. So let's now take a look at how the body responds to the trauma and the stress of bereavement. It may give you a better understanding of why things can go so terribly wrong.

Chapter Two
How the body copes with bereavement

I MENTIONED IN my introduction that the body responds to bereavement by manufacturing several compounds; it releases these compounds into the bloodstream so that we can cope better with the accompanying stress.

Yet this chemical cocktail didn't work very well for George. He became over-stressed, and his means of coping was to ignore his problems - hardly effective. So let's look closer at what happens to our body during bereavement, and discover why we don't handle stress very well. The more we understand how our body reacts, the better prepared we can be when it happens to us.

Don't worry, I'll keep things relatively simple, I'm a financial planner not a medical doctor! If you want to understand more about stress and how the body reacts to it, there are plenty of good books to read, written by medically qualified people. I've also found Google is also a good source for this kind of information.

Sabre-toothed Tigers

When a person experiences loss, the brain responds by producing Corticotropin-releasing hormone (CRH) - it's a hormone responsible for producing anxiety-like symptoms. It also triggers our fight/flight/freeze response when we're faced with danger. This occurs in the most primitive part of our brain, and was important for when our forebears came face to face with a sabre-toothed tiger.

At the same time, other response chemicals are produced, which also place the body in a state of high alert. The level of these chemicals increases as our stress increases, and results in a highly stimulated central nervous system. It's all very helpful when facing the aforementioned sabre-toothed tiger. But what this is doing is storing up trouble. Our body isn't designed to remain in a heightened state for very long, and when our early ancestors faced danger, they quickly dealt with it or ran away from it.

To ensure we don't remain 'pumped up' for too long, the body responds to increases of CRH by producing cortisone. The cortisone enters the blood stream to reduce the effects of CRH. Unfortunately our system cannot differentiate between bereavement related stress, or the immediate danger of coming face to face with a sabre-toothed tiger. Each triggers the same chemical response.

But because the stress of bereavement stays with us for longer, the brain keeps on producing more Corticotropin-releasing hormone. So to counter this, the body produces more cortisone (I've simplified things somewhat). This leads to high levels of cortisone remaining in the blood stream, over a much longer period than the body can cope with. And that's not good.

High levels of cortisone over long periods are dangerous. Eventually it can affect our immune system and we become susceptible to illness. The body's response to stress slowly begins to work against us. Among the first things affected are our natural biological rhythms - sleeping and eating patterns are affected, along with digestion, metabolism, and circulation. Even breathing can become difficult.

Then we might lose coordination - meaning we stumble more easily - and we lose our ability to concentrate. Even simple tasks appear difficult, and we quickly become tired.

Medical research has also shown there are several diseases that can be connected to grief, including: cardiovascular disorders, cancer, pneumonia, and diabetes. To that list you can also add: high blood pressure, chronic depression, alcoholism, drug dependency and malnutrition. We underestimate the devastating effects of bereavement at our peril.

Bereavement affects us emotionally and physically, and the longer we remain stressed, the greater the chance of becoming ill. Stress will exacerbate existing medical conditions, as well as triggering new ones. So what is to be done?

Taking better care of yourself

Bereavement is a difficult time. Yet simply acknowledging this is an important step toward prevention of illness. Being aware of stress, and the probable changes to our eating and sleeping patterns, will itself reduce stress. Also, knowing we are likely to experience lethargy, restlessness, and a lack of physical energy will help us, simply by being aware.

Apart from an awareness of physiological changes, we should acknowledge and outwardly express our emotions. It's simply wrong to try to control our emotions by bottling them inside. This only increases stress and tension. The knock-on effect is an increased likelihood of physical and mental illness (remember George's depression). By the same token, eating poorly, skipping exercise and not sleeping, all add to our stress levels.

Unfortunately, most people will experience some form of illness following the death of a loved one. And in the majority of cases this will be a direct result of long-term stress.

Whilst bereavement on its own is difficult enough to deal with, we should also be aware that is often accompanied by other stressful situations. Often there are financial worries and uncertainties, pushing our stress levels off the scale. Over time we may also experience cracks in relationships with others, causing us to feel alone and isolated, and adding to our stress.

With stress piled on top of stress, is there any wonder body and mind suffers and breaks down?

Stress is a silent killer, and we need to get better at handling it. That means taking better care of ourselves both physically and mentally. Nourishment, exercise, and rest - along with empathetic friends and a shoulder to cry on - are crucial to surviving the stress of bereavement and remaining in good shape.

Chapter Three
Don't leave them financially vulnerable

ON DEATH, EVERYTHING stops. Income ceases, bank accounts are frozen, and nothing moves until probate is granted. I've even come across situations where the deceased was a primary credit card user, and the surviving spouse a named card user. She found her credit card immediately cancelled, leaving her with no means of paying for anything.

So stop for a moment and think: if you were to die today, how would your dependants live?

- Is there sufficient money to meet their basic needs? I don't mean a luxurious lifestyle, but enough to ensure food, shelter, heating and light?
- Do you know where their income will come from?
- Is there a mortgage, and will it be repaid?
- Or must they sell the family home to pay the bills?
- Will they even have enough money to meet any immediate costs?

The following story brings home these points much better than I can.

Natalie and James

I was working in my office one Saturday morning when the phone rang. I don't usually go to the office at the weekend so I thought it was unlikely to be a client. I almost didn't answer it.

But it kept ringing so I picked it up. On the other end was a very distraught woman called Natalie. She was at her wits end and needed some advice. She chose me because my office was nearest to where she lived.

It turned out that six months earlier her husband James, had died. Since then she had been going round and round in circles trying to draw an income from his personal pension. She called me because she was no closer to a solution than she had been at the start.

She wanted to know if I could help her, though she explained she didn't want to see me, because she had no money to pay me. She was wondering whether I would give her some free advice over the phone, which would help her break the deadlock.

Her main worry was her mortgage and her young daughter's school fees. She hadn't been able to pay either of them. She was living a day-to-day existence with whatever income she could generate from her freelance work, but things were becoming more difficult with each passing week.

She was clearly under considerable stress, and I suggested she come and see me anyway, but she refused. So I asked her to outline the pension problem, and then told her what I thought she needed to do. I then told her that if she couldn't make any headway, she should let me try.

I waited all week for her call, but it didn't come. So I went to the office the following Saturday - just in case. Finally she called. She was no further forward, and now the headmaster of her daughter's school was becoming quite anxious about the next term's fees. She didn't have the money. This time she did agree to see me, and it quickly became apparent what the problem was.

With a little knowledge of pensions and investment, James had gone direct to a small firm of pension trustees, who were administering his Self Invested Personal Pension. But because they were not authorised to give any advice, they were unable to tell Natalie what she should do with James' pension. She didn't understand the rules, what her choices were, or what the implications were. She urgently needed the money, but no-one would tell her how to get it.

I suggested the quickest way to resolve things, would be for me to deal with the pension. I could provide the advice that was lacking, and then instruct the trustees what to do. Simply handing the problem to me was a huge relief to Natalie, and I saw the weight of responsibility fall off her shoulders. Now we could start chatting.

I asked her about James, and about how he died. She told me how one Saturday morning James woke up complaining of flu like symptoms - and how he hoped they would pass so he could go to work on Monday morning.

But by the evening his condition was worse, so he took himself off to hospital. It was the last time Natalie saw him alive.

In the early hours of Sunday morning she answered a knock at the front door and saw two policemen standing there. They told her James had gone into a coma at the hospital and subsequently died.

Knowing she was financially vulnerable I asked whether there was any life insurance, either through his employer, or any stand-alone policies. She said James had been in the process of arranging insurance, but he'd been so busy at work he'd left the papers unsigned for several weeks.

Consequently there was no money to repay the mortgage, and nothing to supplement her small amount of savings.

She then talked about the first few weeks following James' death, and how her world simply stopped. She was unable to function, and wanted everyone else's world to stop just like hers had. When she took her daughter to school she would hear other people being happy, and getting on with their lives. It took all her effort to stop herself shouting "STOP". Why couldn't they see she was suffering?

She was angry too. Why could James leave her like that? Why did the hospital let him die? Why her, and why him? What would she do for money? How would she pay the mortgage, the bills, and the school fees?

She woke each morning worrying about the bills that needed paying, and knowing she had too little income to pay them. Then one day she told herself the grieving had to stop. It was a luxury she couldn't afford. She had to work to save her home, pay the bills, and keep her daughter in school - though nothing was guaranteed. Why hadn't James signed the insurance forms?

Bridging the Gap

In countries like the UK and the US, the amount of insurance people have is in decline. Families are less protected than before, despite less available help from the State. The protection industry has always said that insurance policies need to be sold rather than bought voluntarily. And, as we've seen, people do not volunteer themselves to the thought of death or dying.

Personally I'm not a fan of long-term, investment linked, insurance policies, or 'whole of life' contracts. These rarely seem good value to me. In my opinion every pound spent on insurance premiums, is one less pound that could be invested toward your future.

But where there is a financial risk, there is a need to protect it. It should be done as cheaply as possible, using the most appropriate insurance policy to do the job. Adding investment funds or other features is often a waste of money.

Work out what you need to protect, and then protect it - nothing more, nothing less.

In Natalie and James' situation there was a clear need for insurance protection, and it could have been purchased relatively cheaply. Term insurance (sometimes called Temporary insurance) provides a guaranteed level of insurance cover, for an agreed number of years, at a guaranteed premium. That's simple enough to understand.

If affordability is a problem, consider decreasing term insurance (and arguably, if you cannot afford it, the need is even greater). This type of insurance provides a high initial level of cover relative to the premium, because as each year passes, the level of insurance cover reduces. For more details see the section on insurance in Part Two of this book.

A simple insurance policy, for the benefit of Natalie, would have provided her with a sum of money (or a regular income) following James' death. If the policy had been placed inside a simple trust (trusts are also covered in a later chapter) then the money would have been paid without waiting for James' estate to go through probate.

Natalie's story clearly illustrates why basic questions about financial security need to be addressed. If there is insufficient money available on your death to maintain a minimum acceptable lifestyle for your dependants, you need insurance. You should insure your life for an amount sufficient to meet the shortfall. As you get older and generate savings and pensions, the need for insurance decreases. But until then there is a risk.

Take Some Action

Now, without trying to be too accurate, write down how much money would be available to your dependants if you died today (in my experience, waiting for accurate numbers leads to procrastination).

- What money would they receive from any pensions you have?
- Would there be any lump sums from existing insurance policies?
- Do you have any death in service benefits from employment?
- What about the value of any assets already owned?
- Are these subject to any mortgages or loans?
- How much income could these assets generate?
- For how long?

What about the effects of inflation?

At the beginning of this chapter I mentioned the widow who had her credit card cancelled when her husband died. To avoid a similar situation occurring you may wish to consider establishing individual credit card accounts instead of having a primary card holder and a secondary user. This has two benefits If you have a joint credit card with your spouse, and you are named as the primary card holder, then consider establishing individual credit card accounts. This has two benefits 1) the credit card of the surviving spouse will not be cancelled and 2) the surviving spouse builds up a credit history in their own name which is useful at a time when spending may be erratic and other sources of income also being affected.

Chapter Four
Why making a Will is Important

IT SURPRISES ME how many people don't have a valid or up-to-date Will - particularly among the lawyers I've met! And here's my confession; when I started writing this chapter I realised that my own was invalid. I'd drawn up a Will many years ago, but I'd subsequently remarried, and that made it invalid.

But is not having a Will such a big deal?

Well, if you die without making a Will you have no control over who gets what from your estate. And it creates more unnecessary problems for your dependants. It could also mean your estate pays more inheritance tax than it needs to.

Whichever way I look at it, there are no conceivable advantages in not making a Will.

But if you haven't got one, you're not alone. It is estimated that that more than 30 million UK adults don't have one - that's nearly half the entire population. The proportion varies with age, with almost 9 out of 10 people under the age of 35 without a Will. Whereas only 1 in 3 people over 55 are without a Will.

According to research done by the financial and legal advice search website unbiased.co.uk, apathy is the number one reason for not having a valid Will.

'Will Apathy' means many people will die 'intestate' - which is the legal term given to people who die without a valid Will. In these situations it's the government that decides how your estate is divided. And if there are no recognised heirs, the government will take the lot – equivalent to 100% inheritance tax.

So, even if you have no heirs, and don't like the idea of paying everything to the State, you could consider leaving your money to a charity instead? This is something you can easily arrange via a Will - indeed some charities are prepared to help and advise people about Wills, provided the charity is named as a beneficiary.

However, if you die intestate leaving a spouse, children, or other relatives, then they will receive the money in accordance with a set of rules determining who gets what. In the United Kingdom the rules differ depending where the deceased lived: be it England and Wales; Scotland; or Northern Ireland (there is more information in chapter 13). Many people wrongly assume everything will automatically go to their spouse, but the rules may dictate otherwise.

Her husband refused to make a Will

Several years ago I became friendly with Graham and Elsa, a couple who frequented my local pub. Graham was on his second marriage and now enjoying retirement, Elsa, a few years younger was not yet ready to stop work, and she worked part-time. It suited them both.

He'd worked hard throughout his life, eventually building a small business in the North of England, and it gave him a reasonable lifestyle. He'd since transferred the business to his son (from a previous marriage) but the arrangement was such that he continued to draw an income from the business. He had no pension. He also enjoyed the use of several assets still owned by the business.

In effect the business was now supporting two families instead of one, however the turnover hadn't doubled.

I wasn't sure how secure (or indeed how legal) all of this was, but I didn't question things as we only knew each other socially. When it did occasionally crop up in conversation Graham would quickly change the subject.

Then, one day, I heard from Elsa that Graham had been diagnosed with cancer - and it was terminal. Elsa was worried about what would happen when Graham passed away - our occasional conversations had raised concerns that things might not be as secure as they could be. She asked me to talk to Graham about taking some advice regarding their situation.

Initially he was reluctant to talk, but over the following weeks he opened up a bit. I found out that Graham didn't have a Will, and that he didn't believe in them. No amount of pleading from me was going to change that. Graham firmly believed in his family, and told me his son would ensure Elsa was taken care of. He told her she needn't worry.

But Elsa did worry. Relations between her and Graham's children were 'cool' and she feared there would be problems once Graham passed away.

The more she tried to talk to him, the more intractable he became. As Graham's condition became worse, the more they argued about money and Elsa's financial security. Soon the stress became intolerable. Graham was dealing with chemotherapy whilst coming to terms with his imminent death, and Elsa was losing her husband whilst worrying about her future.

I talked to Graham and Elsa on their own as it seemed easier to discuss things with them individually. I'd hoped to persuade Graham that it was important he made proper provision for Elsa, but just as I thought we were making some headway, things took a turn for the worse.

Graham's doctor told him the treatment wasn't working. Time was now against him and he should start saying his goodbyes. The news hit Graham hard, and his condition quickly deteriorated. In just a few days he was admitted to hospital for the final time, and soon went into a coma. He passed away a few days later.

In the final days I'd become Elsa's de-facto representative, spending a lot of time with her at the hospital. I'd been listening to conversations between her and her stepchildren, and knew things would become messy.

Battle lines were drawn even before the funeral. Then, shortly after the funeral, Elsa found that the income had stopped. Although Graham's property was never their marital home she thought it still belonged to Graham, but she discovered it had been transferred into his son's name several years earlier. This was a shock; what she thought was an asset, wasn't even hers, and was now security against a business loan.

Despite a seemingly comfortable lifestyle Graham and Elsa owned very little. Apart from a few pieces of furniture, Elsa could carry almost everything she owned in a couple of large suitcases.

Graham had always believed his son would 'do the right thing' by Elsa. Unfortunately his judgment was clouded by an overarching distrust of professional advice (and a reluctance to pay their fees) and anyone else outside the family.

The money Graham saved by not paying for professional advice was dwarfed by the legal fees incurred by Elsa, and Graham's children. Alas there's no happy ending. Elsa's grief turned to anger, which in turn became bitterness. She found herself virtually homeless, without a pension, and returning to work full-time at an age most people start winding down.

A lot of business people say to me "my business is my pension" and as a business owner I understand why they say that. But what's often missed is the regular withdrawal of profits to build financial security **outside** the business. Then, if something then goes wrong inside the business, there's some financial security to fall back on.

Graham was proud of the business he built, but he hadn't built financial security, at least not for Elsa. Once he passed away, there was nothing to show she had any share in the business, or in any of the other assets. His agreement with his son was based on blood being thicker than water, and nothing else.

Graham and Elsa's story highlights the additional problems that can occur with business ownership on death. Businesses have additional complications (particularly family businesses), and I'll look at these in more detail in a later chapter.

We'll never really know why Graham avoided giving Elsa the security she needed. It wouldn't have cost much for a solicitor to draw up a simple Will. Instead he relied on family, believing his son would look out for everyone. I've met several people like Graham, people who like to be in control, and do things 'their way'. They think the law applies to other people, and not to them, but their mistakes cost other people dearly.

When it came to relations between Elsa and his children, Graham buried his head in the sand. He didn't want to acknowledge a rift between them, so did nothing to provide for Elsa in the event of his death.

A handshake isn't a legal document

Where there are children from previous marriages, things won't always turn out the way we hope. As much as we want to believe that everybody will respect your wishes, something will invariably go wrong. It is always safest to have your wishes legally recorded, and not on a handshake.

It is said that solicitors make more money dealing with contested Wills and estates than they do from drafting Wills. On that basis, who will be the biggest beneficiaries of your estate; the taxman, the legal profession, or your dependants and heirs? It's an easy problem to solve.

Things to consider

Making a Will should be mandatory, but alas it isn't. Until such time it is, here are some questions for you to consider:-

- Do you have a Will?
- Is it valid (was it correctly signed and witnessed)?
- Where is it kept?
- Do your executors know where it is?
- When was your Will last reviewed?

- Have you divorced or remarried since it was last drawn up?

- Does it reflect your current situation and wishes?

- Does it take into account all your assets, wherever they are situated?

- Do you have any overseas assets?

- Have you made a Will in the jurisdiction those assets are situated?

Chapter Five
How to Give Control to Someone Else

IF WE'RE DISCUSSING Wills we should also briefly mention Lasting Powers of Attorney (LPAs). LPAs are used when people no longer have mental capacity to make their own decisions, particularly with regard to things like healthcare, welfare, and financial matters.

When I talk about mental capacity, I simply mean having the capacity to make decisions. It is worth remembering that you can only set up a power of attorney if you have mental capacity to do so. For this reason it makes sense to deal with this at the same time as dealing with your Will.

People often think LPAs are only used when someone suffers from dementia, but there are other circumstances when they are useful to have. People dying because of Terminal Illness often reach the stage where they need to give control to other members of the family.

Similarly an accident may leave someone unable to make their own decisions, perhaps because they're in a coma. In these circumstances it might be preferable for the family to have a legal authority to look after that person's affairs.

It's necessary because without that authority, the State steps in. With an LPA in place it means the family (or friends and legal representatives) can retain control of important decisions about money and welfare etc.

I won't go into too much detail here, other than to briefly outline what LPAs are, as more information can be found in a later chapter.

The Basics

Let us begin with a simple power of attorney, which gives someone the authority to act on your behalf. These are relatively common, particularly among the housebound, who may want to give authority for someone to go to the bank on their behalf (though less so with the increase in internet banking).

Another example might be a student taking a gap year overseas. Giving a temporary power of attorney to their parents, would allow the parents to make transactions on the student's behalf.

A power of attorney doesn't actually make someone a joint account holder, and they don't have ownership of your accounts. It only allows them to do things on your behalf, and only in accordance with the wording contained within the power of attorney.

Losing Mental Capacity

But there is a problem with an ordinary power of attorney if you subsequently lose mental capacity. In this situation it is no longer valid. So if you want someone to continue to make decisions, or take action on your behalf, you need a Lasting Power of Attorney.

If you've previously been involved with looking after someone's affairs you may have come across an Enduring Power of Attorney (EPA). Existing EPAs are still valid, but no new ones can be created, as they have been replaced by Lasting Power of Attorney.

I mainly come across Lasting Powers of Attorney arranged between elderly parents and their children. They may have been in existence for several years, but typically only become effective when the parent goes into a residential or nursing home (usually the latter).

Things to consider

- Do you already have a Lasting (or Enduring) Power of Attorney?

- If not, what would happen to you if you became mentally incapacitated?

- Who do you want making important decisions on your behalf?

- Would you prefer different people to make decisions about health and welfare, versus financial decisions?

Chapter Six
Introducing Trusts

IN THE LATE 1990s I used to facilitate study groups for other financial advisers on the subject of taxation and trusts. The groups were organised to help prepare for exams that eventually led to a chartered level qualification, so they were quite demanding. I found that both subjects caused as many headaches for advisers as they do for anyone else!

It doesn't help that the United Kingdom has one of the most complex tax regimes in the world, and other Western nations are not far behind - tax collection and tax avoidance are complicated businesses.

One tax that many people find iniquitous is inheritance tax. To avoid paying more inheritance tax than necessary, people will often place part of their wealth into a variety of trust arrangements. But these can also be complicated, and often lead to unintended consequences many years after they have been established.

Trusts are an unusual beast, and have evolved their own law and language, so it might be worth spending a little time looking at how they have evolved.

Are trusts only for the wealthy?

Trusts are widely misunderstood, and many people are mistakenly of the impression they are the preserve of the wealthy. But I suspect most of us would be surprised to learn that we're already beneficiaries under one or more trust arrangements.

Most pension schemes are established, and operate under trust law; and if you've ever invested in a unit trust, well, the clue is in the name. Trusts are far more prevalent than we might imagine, and they can be very useful when making financial arrangements that survive after our death.

The Romans and the Crusades

Aspects of trust law stretch back as far as the Romans, who developed the concept of "testamentary trusts' or Will trusts. A Will trust is simply a trust created on a person's death, and which is specified in their Will.

The Romans, however, had not developed a concept whereby trusts could be created by the living. These are called *inter vivos* (living) trusts and they were developed by the English. Oh dear, the language is already sounding quite archaic - but here's why.

We have to go back to medieval times, which was when the concept of trusts as we understand them today, was first developed. In the 12th and 13th centuries when English landowners went off to fight in the Crusades, they needed a legal framework that allowed them to convey ownership of their lands in their absence. The new legal owner would manage the lands, and collect feudal rents while the Crusader was away fighting.

The understanding was that ownership would be conveyed back to the Crusader on their return. And if they didn't return (because they'd been killed), the property was meant to be held 'on trust' for the benefit of the original landowner's heirs and successors.

But because the law at the time wasn't robust enough to enforce the agreement, so some legal owners refused to return the lands. But the law subsequently evolved as disgruntled landowners petitioned the Lord Chancellor for the return of their property. This legal framework became what we now recognise as trust law - and was developed under common law stretching back over 800 years.

Under a trust, the original landowner passed his property to the new legal owner, who held it for the benefit of the original owner. The legal owner was compelled to convey the lands back to the original owner when requested. The Crusader, the original owner, was known as the beneficiary, and the legal owner was known as the trustee.

OK, that's about as far as I'm going with the history of trusts, but there is further explanation later, in Part Two of this book. For now I want to briefly look at how trusts can be used in financial planning - particularly for estate planning and inter-generational transfers of wealth (passing assets to younger generations).

Trusts designed for inheritance tax mitigation

Often, when reviewing the existing financial arrangements of older widows, I'm confronted by 'yellowing' trust documents, for trusts that were previously established for inheritance tax purposes. These were typically arranged when both spouses were alive, and often the surviving spouse has lived longer than the original planning anticipated.

I'll explain what I mean by describing Shirley, whose situation is by no means unique, but just happens to be a recent case I have dealt with. After I've talked about Shirley, the subsequent few paragraphs briefly describe two popular trust arrangements used for inheritance tax planning.

Both are useful when used correctly, but people have run into problems where life expectancy of the surviving spouse has been severely underestimated. This results in large capital sums sitting inside a trust, whilst the surviving spouse struggles to maintain their standard of living. Not dissimilar to the problem that was about to hit Shirley when I first met her.

Shirley's Dilemma

Shirley was referred to me because she was concerned about inheritance tax. She already had some inheritance tax plans, which had been arranged by her and her now deceased husband, some twenty years before. She wanted to look at the possibility of doing something similar, but without losing any of the income her investments were giving her.

In addition to the income she received from her widow's pension and her own moderate investment portfolio, she was also receiving an 'income' from the two inheritance tax friendly trust arrangements that had been established. The 'income' from the trusts generated almost one third of her total income.

Her immediate concern was the value of her estate, which was still well over the inheritance tax threshold. She was considering setting up similar inheritance tax schemes with part of her portfolio, so that she could continue receiving the income, but placing the capital outside her estate.

Yet when we looked at the inheritance tax schemes that Shirley was involved in, we saw that her right to the 'income' was about to cease. The result was that in a couple of years one third of her 'income' was going to stop. The schemes that she and her husband had established were "gift and loan" arrangements; and the money that had been loaned to the trusts had almost all been repaid. It wasn't really 'income' at all, but a return of the original capital.

Needless to say, this presented a completely different problem, and instead of worrying about a potential future inheritance tax bill, Shirley's focus was now on ensuring she had sufficient income to maintain her lifestyle. What had seemed like a good idea almost twenty years before was turning into a major headache.

Their original planning whilst in their early 60s had not considered the husband's early death, which resulted in her pension income falling by half. Inflation had taken its toll over twenty years, and Shirley was still in extremely good health - there was no reason to think she wouldn't be around for another twenty years!

The Gift and Loan Scheme

These schemes are designed for people who wish to gift away the future growth of their investments, but retain access to the original capital.

It works by establishing a discretionary trust (generally making a gift of £100) and then making an interest free loan of a larger amount of capital to trustees. Because the larger sum is loan, it is repayable though people generally choose to receive a regular annual return of capital, typically at a rate of 5% of the original loan amount.

The capital is invested by the trustees, who incidentally have been chosen by you, and any investment growth earned by that capital belongs to the trust rather than belonging to your estate.

The problems I have experienced are usually where the original capital has been fully repaid (take twenty years to be repaid at a rate of 5% per year) and the 'income' then ceases. Added together, this loss of income, coupled with the effect of inflation, and an already reduced widow's pension, hits the surviving spouse particularly hard.

Often the surviving spouse has no recollection that the 'income' is really only a return of capital, and is not usually aware the annual 'income' will stop at some point. It's not hard to see why this might come as a nasty surprise, as these arrangements may well have been made twenty years beforehand.

We underestimate life expectancy at our peril. I've met enough elderly widows to learn that running out of capital is a bigger worry to them than their estate having to pay inheritance tax.

The Discounted Gift Plan

Another fairly common arrangement I come across is the 'Discounted Gift Plan'. In a similar way to a 'gift and loan' scheme, if you want to give away capital to reduce the potential amount of inheritance tax on your estate, yet still need to draw an income from the capital, you might consider a Discounted Gift Plan.

A Discounted Gift Plan is designed to provide an 'income' from a gift of capital, and provide an immediate reduction (a discount) in the value of your estate. The level of the discount is calculated based on the amount of income being taken, prevailing interest rates, and your life expectancy.

Because the potential discount reduces with age, these plans are more attractive the younger you are at the outset. This again creates problems around making long term projections about future inflation, income needs, and life expectancy, and my experience has been that people tend to underestimate all three.

I'll go into the basic mechanics of this plan (and also the 'gift and loan' scheme) in Part Two. For now I simply want to draw your attention to the potential problems of trying to forecast income and capital needs as far ahead as twenty years or so.

Keeping Pension Funds outside the Estate

I'm not 'anti-trusts' by the way, used correctly they can be very beneficial in mitigating inheritance tax. They can be particularly useful with regard to death benefits arising from a deceased spouse's pension scheme.

Recently, one of my clients asked what the situation would be if he died and his pension funds were transferred to his spouse. He was concerned that pension funds that were currently not subject to inheritance tax, would subsequently become part of his spouse's estate and subsequently be subject to inheritance tax at 40%.

Death benefits from a pension scheme are typically distributed to a surviving spouse (and/or other eligible beneficiaries). As a result the death benefits become the property of the surviving spouse, and subsequently, on their death may be subject to inheritance tax - even if death occurs shortly after the death of the pension scheme member.

We've been recommending our clients to use a "Spousal Bypass Trust" as a solution. This arrangement avoids death benefits passing directly to a spouse, meaning the death benefits will not form part of the spouse's estate.

Of course, it is highly likely the surviving spouse will need access to the capital at some time in the future, so they will be listed as a potential beneficiary of the trust. Typically the trust would make an interest free loan to the surviving spouse, which would be repayable on their death, thus creating a debt against their estate, reducing the liability to inheritance tax even further.

Spousal bypass trusts can be used with most pension arrangements, including occupational pension schemes that have lump sum death in service benefits. There are some older style personal arrangements where they cannot be used - Section 32 Buyout plans and Retirement Annuity contracts.

By establishing a spousal bypass trust, the value of the pension scheme does not become liable to inheritance tax on the death of the member's spouse. The member also retains some control by providing a 'letter of guidance' to the trustees outlining who the preferred beneficiaries are, of any death benefits to be paid.

Clearly this is something that can only be done when you're alive, so if you're reading this and thinking it sounds like a good idea, then please, take some action. But make sure you take professional advice.

Recent changes to the taxation of pension benefits on death mean that a spousal bypass trust may not always be the most beneficial option, particularly if the pension was already in payment at the time of death.

Summary and Questions

Even for professional advisers, trusts can present a challenge, particularly when dealing with older trusts established under a different tax regime. Many people I meet have some difficulty with the concept of money sitting within a trust not belonging to them. Instead it belongs to the trustees, who hold it 'on trust' for the beneficiaries benefit.

The problems that I see most often are where packaged trust schemes have been used without sufficient consideration of the long term needs of a surviving spouse. It really requires someone to run some long-term cash-flow projections, which also include modeling scenarios such as the early demise of one or other spouse.

If you already have one or more of these inheritance tax schemes, or are contemplating using one, it is well worth reviewing the long term effects of placing capital outside the estate this way.

- What assumptions have you used regarding life expectancy? Many of us underestimate life expectancy, leading to a long term reduction in our standard of living as our income declines.

- Have you fully considered the effects of a reduced pension income for the surviving spouse?

- What assumptions have you made regarding inflation? Over time even the real value of pension income reduces as pension increases rarely keep up fully with inflation.

- Is your planning driven more by potential inheritance tax savings than by the long term sustainability of your standard of living?

- Have you thought about the effects and the costs of long term care?

Chapter Seven
Thinking about Investments

THE MAIN REASON people seek my help is to get investment advice. Sometimes this is wrapped up in other financial products like pensions or individual savings accounts (ISAs), but generally people are looking at ways to invest their capital.

If I'm advising a widow for the first time, there is often a mixture of emotions bubbling under the surface that I need to be aware of. Fear, apprehension, embarrassment and distrust are generally high on the list, and sometimes these will deter someone from taking advice for quite a long time.

When they eventually overcome their inertia and seek advice, I find there's often a lot of time spent fixing problems that have compounded over a relatively long period of time.

A cycle of fear and embarrassment

In several cases where I've been advising widows, I've witnessed a cycle of emotions they've been through. I've since discussed this with several widows, and they've told me how they went through similar cycles, or variations of it. It's not the same for everyone of course, but I thought it worth sharing, because I have observed this on several occasions.

As I've mentioned before, (and perhaps it's a generational thing) many women seem to take a back seat when it comes to making investment decisions. A couple's investments are often the husband's responsibility - though as some academic studies have confirmed, men don't necessarily make better investors!

However, when he dies, all the responsibility passes over to the widow. But as we've already learned, during bereavement she's under so much stress she's not ready to make serious decisions - least of all investment decisions that were previously her husband's responsibility.

But there are immediate worries about money, for example; about where her income will come from. This can easily create a sense of fear about making the wrong decision. The sense of fear sometimes leads to inertia, and so the decisions are deferred - until the fear is replaced by embarrassment.

Embarrassment is present because they know they've left things for too long. Also they perceive they have a lack of knowledge, so they'll ignore things a little longer.

Eventually something happens to overcome this embarrassment and inertia. They experience a different fear. It could be a significant fall in the stock-market, or something occurring in the wider economy, but eventually their fear becomes so great it overcomes everything else.

But their emotional problems aren't over. They're often apprehensive of what they might discover, and can be distrustful of advisers - yet they realise they must do something, the status quo cannot continue.

For people in this situation, financial advice cannot be hurried. They need time to develop a degree of trust, and to understand what is being presented to them, particularly if their problems require radical solutions.

As mentioned earlier, this emotional cycle will not be experienced by every bereaved person, but I've seen it often enough to believe it affects a significant number of people to a greater or lesser degree.

Sometimes it's easier to switch advisers

There's an interesting statistic I recently discovered: according to academic research, a widow will change investment advisers, on average 17 months following the death of her husband.

If my clients are typical clients, I would concur with that 17 month timescale, though admittedly when I first read the research I was sceptical. I didn't believe it was as short as 17 months, so I looked through my own files for evidence, and in the end had to agree that the findings were likely to be true.

In fact, one of my first widow client's (Judith) actually appointed me 17 months and 3 days following her husband's death. This is what she told me about why she left her previous advisers.

To start with she said she didn't really know them, because her husband had taken care of most of the investment decisions. It was probably her own fault, but at the time she just wasn't that interested. And for a while after her husband died, she wasn't really 'with it' but eventually decided she needed to be involved. But from the very first meeting, she felt she was being talked down to.

Her 'account manager' would say things like "don't worry, we'll take care of things" but she did worry. She relied on the investment portfolio for much of her income, and the capital gave her a feeling of financial security. She was worrying about the future, and they kept telling her not to. No doubt they thought they were being helpful, but to Judith it came across as condescending.

And when they did talk to her, the language and terminology was alien. No-one was making it their responsibility to help her understand. She would hear comments like "this is what Peter would have done" and immediately her hackles would rise - she was itching to scream "Peter isn't here anymore, so would someone please explain it to me".

Eventually she decided it would be easier to move her investment portfolio, and give it to someone who would at least explain things to her, even if it didn't perform better. She knew there would be costs involved, and there was no guarantee that the investments would even continue to perform as they had. But she wasn't comfortable staying where she was, so she left.

The portfolio was transferred to my firm, and we've spent several years working with Judith. We had regular meetings with her for the first 18 months or so, until she felt comfortable that she knew what we were doing. Now she only wants to see us once a year. She's busy doing other things, meeting friends and travelling. She says she's comfortable, and that we're approachable. Most importantly, she doesn't feel afraid to call us and ask a silly question.

I cannot help thinking that if the previous company had invested just a little more time talking with Judith, she wouldn't have moved. There would have been continuity, and she would have avoided any fees and upheaval of changing advisers. Their mistake was not to have established a relationship with her before Peter's death.

Judith's experience is not an isolated one, it happens frequently. Ironically, when firms lose clients like Judith, they end up spending far more time, money and effort trying to attract new clients. This doesn't serve anyone well, it's costly, inefficient, and creates more upheaval than is really necessary.

Build support early

In my firm we decided we wouldn't work with a couple if we didn't have at least one meeting a year where both of them were present. This annual meeting isn't about charts, graphs and statistics, but instead reviews financial goals, and whether they're on track. We also want to provide reassurance that we're looking out for them, should anything happen. We don't want to become strangers.

I talk about this at my first meeting, and I explain the problems I've seen other widows go through. I stress the importance of developing a relationship with both of them, so that we get to know each other. The reason being; if one of them died the surviving spouse knows who to call.

From the beginning we work toward creating that 'trusted team': the people who will help pick up the pieces, and make sure the right things are done. If someone doesn't know who we are, it'll lead to unnecessary fear and trepidation, just at the point the bereaved needs absolute faith in the people around them.

I get a warm feeling when I hear a spouse tell me that if her husband dies I'll be one of the first people she calls. She knows we've already got 'Plan B' to make sure the finances are going to be OK. Everything has been discussed beforehand, so there are no hidden surprises. We know where future income will come from, and where all the investments are. Of course, and more importantly, they know.

Changing advisers can be a costly matter. And if you're not thinking straight, you could end up choosing the wrong ones, and that can be expensive. The real lesson here is to build trusted relationships with advisers that will survive the trauma of bereavement. Not only do they help you build a robust financial strategy for whilst you're alive, they also assist in the transition following bereavement. Ideally there will be a strategy already mapped out.

A small fortune often starts with a big one!

Several years ago I was asked to advise someone who was frantic with worry about money. Several years before there had been a succession of deaths within a very short space of time and she'd inherited a large sum. Back in the early nineties this inheritance would have provided her with an income of approximately £150,000 each year - had it been managed prudently.

By the time I met her, however, the value of her investments would barely support an income of £50,000 a year. What happened to the other millions I wondered?

It turned out that over the years there had been a succession of advisers, all with different ideas, and all keen to stamp their mark on her investment portfolio. Each time she changed advisers there was a new round of initial charges, and often a lot of buying and selling. In some cases as much as 5% of the capital was 'lost' in fees and commissions each time she changed.

When I looked through the history it became obvious that she had lost a significant amount of money on unnecessary switching costs. Those five-percents soon add up. On top of that she'd received some diabolical investment advice.

For example, one adviser encouraged her to sell several residential properties in London, just before the long bull-run in London property prices. She missed out on a property rally that would have more than doubled her money, and provided her with a decent rental income. When that didn't work out she again changed advisers - the next ones weren't much better.

They advised her to invest in the dot com bubble, and again she lost a significant amount of money. But regardless of her dwindling fortune, she was still spending at an equivalent rate of £150,000 a year and no-one was telling her to stop. Instead they were setting up expensive offshore structures, and the additional fees and charges became another drain on the portfolio.

When I met her the first thing I did was to show how her spending was making the problem worse. If she didn't drastically reduce her expenditure she would run out of money in less than 10 years - the problem was, she had a life expectancy of more than 20 years. Reining in her spending wasn't an easy thing to do, and it took several attempts, but eventually she cut it by almost two thirds.

But still it wasn't quite enough, so she decided to downsize her property. This would reduce her costs, and free up additional capital. Then we helped her build a simple portfolio based on stocks and bonds, to produce a reasonable level of income, and the prospect of some capital growth. There was nothing too fancy or complicated.

Soon we'd helped her to understand what she really needed to know. She'd started budgeting, and she took some personal responsibility, and took control of her finances. Eventually everything became simple enough that she didn't need as much hand holding. Our role was reduced which also reduced the fees she paid us each year. I'd say that was a success. I just wish we'd got to her earlier.

Over many conversations with her, I'd learned she'd been very naive when she'd inherited the money. She left the first investment managers because she didn't feel she belonged there. They were part of the city 'establishment' - and she wasn't. She felt they were constantly talking down to her. With hindsight, they were probably the best placed to look after her money, but there was no relationship - and as I've discovered, a relationship is often more important than being the best investment manager!

Not everyone is a DIY investor

But it's not just the switching of advisers that creates problems. We are plagued by other emotions that bubble up to the surface, and these can also create problems.

One frequent situation I come across is where the husband has been a D.I.Y. investor, making all the investment decisions on his own. Often the widow doesn't really know what they're invested in, or why. And because he's been a D.I.Y. investor there's rarely an existing adviser relationship; so when disaster strikes, she's on her own.

Suddenly the widow finds she's responsible for making investment decisions, and realises she's out of her depth. She has no familiarity or understanding with what's involved, and she doesn't really know who to ask. Many widows I've worked with have said they've been embarrassed about their lack of knowledge, and their embarrassment stops them seeking advice. It's a vicious circle.

So for a while it's easier for them to bury their head in the sand. This might continue for several years, but at some point their financial worries will eventually overcome their embarrassment. But several years is really a lifetime in today's financial world, and often it's an impending financial disaster that pushes them to obtain help.

It's perfectly OK to do your own thing, handling your own investments and financial planning, but it's not for everyone. Establishing a back-up plan whereby you can hand over your affairs to someone you can trust is a responsible thing to do.

I recently took a call from a doctor who had been diagnosed with cancer. He said he'd been managing his financial affairs for most of his life, but his wife would need some advice once he passed away. He didn't want to hand over the reins just yet, but did want to develop a relationship with someone. Someone who could take care of his wife's financial planning needs when he was no longer able to.

Emotional ties get in the way

Even when we're in a good frame of mind, emotion will often get in the way of making sensible investment decisions. We've already seen the trouble emotions bring, when trying to make rational decisions during bereavement. But even in the post bereavement phase our decisions will be influenced by our emotions, including emotions around guilt and loss.

Many people will build up a significant share holding in their employer's company, through stock options and the like. Apart from a concentration of investment risk, this can bring other issues to the fore. For many widows, inheriting these shares is rather like inheriting his legacy. The shares are a tangible connection to their husband, and they'd feel a loss if they were to sell them.

This is a difficult emotion to overcome, and often painful too. In the same way that a widow may want to keep her husband's clothes, she may also want to keep shares in the company he spent so many years working for.

The same can be said for any other assets he may have accumulated. If he was a keen investor the widow may be reluctant to sell shares, even if he was an active trader himself.

I haven't found an easy way of dealing with this situation though time is usually the key. I firmly believe that if couples were able to discuss this kind of thing beforehand they would find a solution.

Summary

This has been a big chapter to deal with, and we've hardly scratched the surface. But what have we learned so far?

From my perspective, it's important for everyone to be involved in the financial planning process. There is tremendous comfort in knowing there's someone to turn to when disaster strikes.

It's even better if everyone's "on the same page" with regard to Plan B. Trust is an important factor, and if it isn't already there when someone's coming to terms with bereavement, it's too late - trust must already exist. So take steps to create a trusted team around you.

If you're the type of person who prefers to handle their own investments, think about who would take over if you weren't there. It's quite possible the portfolio would have different objectives to meet if you passed away. Hanging on to growth stocks might not be a good idea if income suddenly becomes a priority. It's important for your dependants to know this, so that they don't hang onto inappropriate investments for sentimental reasons.

Financial planning isn't the same as investment management, so just because you manage your own investments, doesn't mean you can't work with a financial planner. They will be part of the trusted team that will be there to assist your dependants when you're not there.

Action Points

There are steps you can take that will make the ongoing administration of investments a little easier, and in some circumstances, reduce future tax liabilities.

- Keep an up-to-date list of every asset and investment you own, whether in your sole name, or jointly held - and make sure the executors of your estate know where it is.

- Keep details of when each investment was purchased (and when sold where appropriate), and details of any dealing costs.

- Keep a record of any income received from investments. Your estate will still be liable for income tax on any investments owned at the date of death.

Chapter Eight
Dealing with Pension issues

WE'VE ALREADY READ about Natalie's problems trying to obtain money from James's pension. In all it took over nine months before she received the money she was entitled to. Part of the delay was because Natalie attempted to do it alone without professional help, but even when I became involved it still took several weeks to get the money released.

Pensions are complicated, and become ever more complicated due to continuous legislative changes brought about by the Treasury and successive governments. For the time being it doesn't look as though pensions will get simpler, this is one area you would benefit from having someone who specialises.

Problems are further complicated by trying to sort out entitlements from a variety of different pension types. It could be pensions in payment, or deferred benefits, private or occupational pensions, or even State pension benefits.

In 'Part Two' you can read about some of the different types of pension that you might be dealing with. But in this section I'm going to look at two unusual pension situations I've been involved with.

Forgotten Plans

I don't know about you, but when I look back over the last ten or even twenty years, time seems to have flown by. It doesn't feel as though much could have changed but when I review my personal circumstances, they've changed almost beyond recognition. The arrangements I made back then only have limited relevance to my situation now. I know I'm not the only one to experience this.

Twenty years ago, Terry gave his pension trustees a "letter of wishes" (sometimes called an "expression of wishes") about where he would like his 'death in service' benefits to go on his death. At the time he couldn't have imagined the problems this would create for Mary, his wife.

I'd met Mary about a year after Terry's death. He'd suffered a fatal heart attack leaving Mary to look after three teenage children. He was in his early fifties and his death was sudden and unexpected. For many families this might have created significant financial problems, but Terry had been a member of his firm's "final salary" pension scheme, which provided generous pension and death benefits.

In only a few weeks Mary received a widow's pension sufficient to maintain a reasonable standard of living. Being natural savers, Terry and Mary had already repaid their mortgage, and had no other debts to worry about - though there were some large school fees due.

The pension scheme also paid a small income to each of their children still in full-time education. It amounted to a few thousand pounds per child, and allowed them to continue their extra-curricular school activities. Financially Mary felt relatively secure, albeit a little squeezed - she still needed to work to supplement her pension income.

Terry's "letter of wishes" requested the pension trustees to distribute any death in service payments as per his instructions in the letter. Twenty years earlier when he'd completed it, both he and Mary both decided the lump sum benefits should be shared equally between their children, with Mary receiving the pension income.

Now, twenty years later, Mary thought this was no longer equitable and wanted the pension trustees to alter the distribution. She didn't want the money for herself, she just felt the younger children were being penalised relative to the oldest child. This was something she strongly believed Terry would have wanted to avoid.

Terry and Mary had agreed their children's education was one of the most important things they could give as a start in life. They had foregone other luxuries to give each child the best education they could. Although it meant there was little scope to help them in other ways (like helping with a deposit on a property) they were of the opinion a good education trumped everything else.

Now that Mary was receiving a reduced income, she could no longer afford to pay the school fees as she and Terry had done. But the death in service money allocated to each child would be more than enough to cover the education costs.

However, the oldest child had almost finished university, meaning his share of the money would not go toward the costs of education (Mary and Terry had covered his costs). Mary believed this was unfair on the younger children. They would essentially be paying for their own education from their trust monies, whereas Terry and Mary had paid all the oldest child's costs.

Mary wanted the pension trustees to divide the payments unequally, so that the younger children received more of the money which would pay for their school and university costs.

At age 25 each child would then receive their share of the remaining money outright, and Mary wanted each child to receive a similar amount to give them a similar start in life. But unless the trustees changed their minds, there would be virtually nothing for the youngest child when she became 25 years old.

After a year Mary had still not been able to convince the trustees to distribute the funds in the way she believed Terry would have wanted. If it wasn't resolved soon Mary would run out of money herself, as she was funding everything from her savings.

She asked me to assist her with a final attempt to change the trustee's decision. I wish I could say we were successful, but despite our best efforts they wouldn't budge. Mary feels strongly her children have been treated differently, and her response has been to change the provisions of her Will so that eventually the imbalance will be redressed.

So, what can we take from this?

The first thing to ask is whether you know what benefits are payable on your death? And who are they be payable to?

If you haven't already, you may wish to provide your pension trustees with a letter of wishes about where you would wish your pension benefits paid on your death. The letter isn't a binding instruction to the trustees (by law it cannot be) but can be a useful guide.

If you have previously provided a letter of wishes you may wish to review its contents and revise it as appropriate. It could be that you gave instructions several years ago and that your circumstances have changed. A regular review of these things doesn't take very long.

Some people arrange for their pension benefits to go into a family trust on their death, for the benefit of a spouse and children. I'll briefly explain this in the later section about trusts.

In the meantime let me tell you about a case I was involved in several years ago. It involved Richard, who'd been diagnosed with an aggressive form of terminal cancer. He wanted to make sure he maximised whatever benefits he could for Ruth, his wife, and this included his preserved occupational pension benefits.

Making the most out of his pension

Richard had once been a teacher, and somewhere in the system there was a preserved pension benefit that would be paid when he turned 60. But cancer meant that Richard wouldn't make it to his sixtieth birthday, he was in his mid-fifties and had less than a year to live.

The year was spent ticking off a number of things in his "Bucket List" whilst he still had the energy, and it also meant he could bring his affairs in order so that financially at least, Ruth would have an easier journey.

When we looked into the benefits available to Ruth we found they were not that great. Certainly they were nowhere near as good as the benefits available to later members of the scheme. The forecast showed that she would probably get a pension equal to a third of the pension Richard would get at age 60. It would also be taxed.

So we looked at other options, and asked the pension trustees for a transfer value. We figured that if the pension transfer value reflected the true value of Richard's preserved benefits, it might be in their best interests to transfer it.

We ran the analysis, and weighing up other factors we decided to transfer the pension, resulting in Richard now having a Personal Pension worth more than half a million pounds.

This opened up the possibility of taking benefits immediately, but we decided against that, there was no immediate need for the money. The legislation meant that when Richard died, provided the personal pension hadn't been used to provide pension benefits (it hadn't) the entire pension fund would pass to Ruth, as a lump sum, entirely tax free.

We calculated that even if Ruth simply invested the money in index linked government bonds, she would have double the income that she would have received from the original pension scheme. Not only that, but the capital was available to pass down to their children on her death. Whereas under the occupational pension, once she died the money would stop.

Summary and Questions

Pensions are rarely straightforward to deal with, the rules are complicated and they keep changing. Things are made worse by different pension schemes having slightly different rules, all within a complex regulatory framework.

But there are some things you can do to make things easier.

- Make a list of all the schemes you are a member of. You may have benefits from previous employers, or old personal pension arrangements.

- If you've moved house and not informed pension trustees of your new details, now's the time to do it.

- If you've married, divorced, or remarried, inform the scheme trustees.

- If you have dependant children, inform the scheme trustees.

- Have you provided the trustees with an up to date letter of wishes?

- Does it reflect your current thoughts about who should receive pension benefits?

- Do you have any Additional Voluntary Contribution schemes?

- Is there any separate Death in Service benefit payable?

- Does it provide an option to increase cover if there's a protection shortfall?

- Do you know what benefits are payable on death?

- When will they be paid?

Chapter Nine
Our Love affair with Property

WE BRITISH LOVE our property, and a significant proportion of our wealth is often tied up in homes; whether it's our main home, a second home, or a rental property. Accordingly, the long term property investor is likely to have a large amount of money tied up in bricks and mortar, often leading to a situation where they're considered 'asset rich, but income poor'.

The 'asset rich, income poor' problem will often be exacerbated by old age. As the purchasing power of pensions decreases through the effects of inflation, and property upkeep costs continue rising, older people will often find they own a large asset that doesn't generate any income. In fact it's often a cash drain.

But we fall in love with our homes, we invest a lot of time, effort and money into our homes, and they often hold fond memories. We have a strong emotional attachment to property that is rarely felt with other forms of investment. Because of this, many people remain in their homes for longer than is financially prudent.

The Problem with Property

The problem with property is that it's simply too big. Most other investments, like shares or government bonds, can be sold piecemeal to meet income or capital needs, but it would be hard to sell small parts of a property to supplement your income. And that assumes you wanted to sell.

But like many other physical assets, property also requires constant upkeep and maintenance. When you're younger and in good health, much of this you can do yourself, but as you get older, or more infirm, you may need to pay others to do this for you. Even the jobs you once considered simple, such as trimming the hedge, eventually end up costing money when you need to employ someone else to do them.

And if the time comes when you need to "tighten your belt" some of these jobs might be ignored, leaving the property to slowly decay, and failing to retain its value compared to similar properties.

Borrowing

One of the biggest attractions of property however, is the ability to borrow money in order to buy it. But in the wrong circumstances this debt becomes a millstone around the neck of a surviving spouse.

We saw in an earlier chapter how Natalie was under considerable strain to maintain mortgage payments because there was no life insurance payout on James' death. With such a long term commitment there is no guarantee that Natalie will hold on to the property. If mortgage rates increase, or she doesn't earn enough income, she may be forced to sell her home to keep her head above water.

Borrowing to fund a property purchase is not risk free, and where there are dependant's welfares at stake, life insurance should be used to ensure they can at least repay the debt on death.

There's a similar situation with buy-to-let properties too. Many people start out buying a rental property with a large mortgage, which will be repaid using the rental income. Their long term aim is to gradually repay the mortgage, and so create a future income stream; as well as some capital appreciation.

However, if death occurs in the early years of ownership, and before the mortgage has been repaid, the surviving spouse finds they're holding an asset that doesn't necessarily pay its way. They are also at risk of rising interest rates, void periods, and even a slump in property prices. These may not be big problems for a couple with a joint income to support them, but following the death of one of them, the situation can quickly change.

Familiarity and Community

As people become older they tend to become more set in their ways, and less willing to change. Living in a property for a long time brings familiarity, we become used to it, and its idiosyncrasies.

We also become part of the local community, building a circle of friends and other people we come to rely on. We establish routines, have our favourite shops, and generally settle into a life that is as hassle free as possible. Uprooting all this becomes a terrible strain; more so the older we are.

So, if we know that we may need to downsize at some point in the future, far better to do it sooner rather than later. Certainly it is easier to achieve if there are two of you, than trying to do it alone. It is said that buying, selling and moving home, is one of the most stressful things we will engage in. It doesn't sound like a good idea to contemplate this later in life, or even worse, during a period of bereavement.

Mixed emotions

I was recently talking with Marion, a widow who owned several properties; a couple of them were let, one was used as a second home, and there was also the main residence. Her husband's priority had been to build a small portfolio of properties, rather than build a pension. As a result she only had a small pension income to live on, but a relatively large amount of money tied up in property, though very little of it was generating any income.

With her husband she had enjoyed a comfortable lifestyle, which they could afford because he continued to earn at high level. He was a barrister, and they spent part of the week in a large London home, and the remainder of the time in their country cottage. He expected to continue working well into his 70s and even into his 80s. Unfortunately he died of a heart problem in his early 60s.

Ideally Marion wanted to remain living in the London home, whilst spending longer periods of time at the cottage. Realistically she knew this was unaffordable; the upkeep costs of the two properties, and her basic living expenses, were greater than the income she was receiving.

The other rental properties did provide a small amount of income, but the properties were not high in value, and the rental yield was relatively small once the upkeep costs were taken into account.

Marion had spent the last couple of years worrying about what to do about the various properties. Should she sell the rental properties, should she let the cottage, should she downsize from the London home? She was undecided, and additionally her children each had different views as to what she should do. All the time she was trying to make her mind up, her cash pile was dwindling as she continued to supplement her low income, and maintain the properties.

The London home and country cottage both contained powerful memories of her husband, so a decision to sell or let was understandably difficult. Marion said if she'd been able to discuss this scenario with her husband before his death, she felt the decision would have been easier.

The Capital Gains Tax Trap

Because property is generally a large, illiquid asset, it makes it harder for investment properties to be managed in a way that minimises capital gains tax.

Over a long period of time property investors can find there's a lot of profit tied up in their asset, which if sold would trigger a large tax bill. But because Capital Gains Tax (CGT) is not payable on death, many people choose to hold on to the property until death wipes out the tax.

But whilst CGT is wiped out on death, inheritance tax is introduced. So there may be limited opportunity to mitigate inheritance tax if you're unwilling to sell a property because of CGT reasons.

Chapter Ten
Business Assets

BUSINESS ASSETS CAN be difficult to unravel following the death of a business owner. Large companies are likely to have formal arrangements to 'buy out' a deceased person's shares or partnership interest. On the other hand, smaller companies, partnerships, and sole traders are less likely to have anything in place.

Typically it's the smaller enterprise where the owner is also likely to take the view that 'my business is my pension' – meaning there's a potential double financial whammy on their death. The business might struggle to continue trading, and any pension benefits may be insufficient to support a bereaved spouse.

If you're in business you should periodically review the arrangements dealing with transfer of ownership on your death. If you haven't yet got any arrangements, then now might be a good time!

Many business people want to leave their business to a spouse, or at least want their spouse to benefit from the value. This is easily done using a Will, and gifting shares in the business to a spouse. But is this the most tax efficient way?

In one situation I recently looked at we wanted to make maximum use of Business Property Relief to reduce the likelihood of inheritance tax being payable in the future.

Stephen and Barbara Plan Ahead

Unlike many of the case studies in this book, I'm happy to report that both Stephen and Barbara are still alive.

Stephen has a small business, which generates significant recurring revenue from 'intellectual property' created over several years. Even if he died there would be a long-term ongoing income from various royalties and other sales. Except for some book keeping and accounting, the business could easily run itself if Stephen wasn't around. It wouldn't be growing of course, but would continue to provide healthy revenues for several years to come.

The nature of the recurring revenue means that the business has a nominal value of nearly two million pounds, if he decided to sell it today. Stephen's previous Will stipulated that on his death, the company and all it's assets would transfer directly to Barbara. As there is no inheritance tax on transfers between spouses this seemed the sensible thing to do.

Our view was that this didn't make best use of Business Property Relief, particularly if Barbara were to die shortly after Stephen. Business Property Relief is granted on qualifying businesses, and means they can be transferred with no inheritance tax liability, even to someone other than a spouse.

We arranged a meeting with their accountant and a solicitor, to outline a plan whereby on Stephen's death, his company shares would be transferred into a trust. No inheritance tax would be payable because the shares qualified for Business Property Relief. Once in the trust, the trustees would decide whether to sell the business, or to continue receiving the recurring income.

Barbara was named as a beneficiary of the trust, as were their children. The trust wording enabled the trust to lend money to Barbara in the form of an IOU. It didn't matter whether the assets were sold and she took capital, or whether she took income as it accumulated. In both cases the money she received would be a loan, and therefore creating a debt on her estate.

As a debt, it means the value of her estate on death will be reduced. This has the effect of lowering the eventual inheritance tax bill. The trust also means their children may also receive capital or income in the future.

Keeping it in the Family

This point about lending assets to his children appealed to Stephen. The ability to exert an element of control even after his death was attractive, and Stephen was keen to protect his wealth and keep it within the family.

Like many parents, he was concerned at what might happen if his children received significant sums of money, only to lose it in the case of divorce. By holding assets in a trust, it becomes possible to lend assets to his children instead of giving outright ownership. This may reduce the likelihood of wealth passing outside the family if his children divorced.

Bear in mind there are no guarantees that the assets are ring-fenced in a divorce, though there is an element of protection over and above not having a trust. But the law is constantly changing and it is crucial to always take legal advice in situations such as this.

Succession

When thinking about the family, there is often the assumption that a family business will automatically pass down the generations. But this cannot be taken for granted these days. Society has changed, and people are more mobile, have different aspirations and expectations. Whilst mum and dad might have been happy to take over the reins of the family business, it isn't necessarily the case today.

There is a point where the future of a family business needs to be discussed with the people who are expected to inherit it. The premature death of a business owner may bring about a difficult situation where the future of the business is uncertain. It might not be pleasant to learn that your offspring have no desire to follow in your footsteps, but better to know now, than for the business to suffer through disagreement after your death.

If you think that conversations about business succession will be too difficult for you to handle alone, there are trained specialists skilled in 'facilitating' difficult family discussions. They can also assist with helping you plan a business succession in a number of circumstances; retirement, partial retirement, ill health or death.

The Problems of Joint Ownership

Of course, not all businesses have a simple ownership structure like Stephen's - he is the sole owner. There are thousands of businesses that have multiple owners, and joint ownership creates additional problems on death.

Some problems may exist within the business, such as the death of a key person, and some would affect the deceased's family and dependants.

If you are a key person, and the business would suffer significantly on your death, you should be considering 'Key Person Insurance' to provide a capital sum available to the business on your death. This could be used to 'buy in' key skills lost on your death - thus safeguarding the interests of the remaining owners, including your dependants.

You should also consider the roles played by the other owners of the business - if any of them are key people, the business should be insuring them for the same reasons outlined above.

But the other consideration I want to look at is how you would deal with your share of the business in the event that you die. If you leave your shares to your spouse (or in trust for her benefit) this can potentially create a number of problems.

The most obvious is what role would the surviving spouse have in the company. The other shareholders may not like the idea of having to find an active role for your spouse, and equally, may not wish to share profits with an inactive shareholder. All things considered it may be better if the other shareholders purchased the shares, thus providing your spouse with a capital sum in exchange for her shareholding in the business.

But unless the remaining shareholders have sufficient capital to purchase the shares they're going to be stuck with a situation they may prefer not to have. The obvious solution is therefore to use life assurance to provide the capital. Structured the right way this would pay a lump sum on a shareholder/

partner's death, providing the money to purchase shares from the deceased's spouse.

I'm over simplifying the situation here, and there are other important considerations that need to be taken into account. For example, any agreement to buy shares from the deceased's spouse must not be a binding agreement between both parties, as this has adverse inheritance tax implications. Typically a 'cross-option' agreement is used, giving one party the option to buy the shares, or the other party the option to sell the shares.

The schemes that do this are referred to as 'shareholder protection' in the case of companies, or 'partnership protection' in the case of partnerships. Involve your accountant and your solicitor when arranging these schemes, so as to ensure the arrangements are wholly appropriate for your company's needs – don't rely on standard insurance company documentation as it is typically a 'one-size fits all' option.

Business Property Relief and Inheritance Tax

Business Property Relief can also be used to relieve the burden of inheritance tax. Purchasing qualifying assets and holding them for at least 2 years, they will be excluded from the estate for inheritance tax purposes. There are several investment firms that will construct portfolios of qualifying shares for investors wishing to save inheritance tax.

Unsurprisingly, schemes that reduce the inheritance tax liability have been increasing in popularity. As the government's rakes in more money from inheritance tax (through freezing the allowances, and a general rise in asset values) the more incentive there is for people to reduce their liability.

Compared to the more traditional inheritance tax planning methods, like using annual gift allowances, or placing money into trust, these schemes can seem attractive. The obvious attractions are that it can speed up the whole process, and you don't have to give up ownership or control.

Making relatively small annual gifts can take a long time to get money out of the estate - the annual gift allowance is only £3,000 per individual. Larger gifts would normally require that you survived 7 years before it was excluded from your estate for inheritance tax purposes. Gifts into certain types of trust can even take up to 14 years before they are wholly excluded from the inheritance tax calculation.

For many people inheritance tax is a real concern; having paid taxes throughout their lives, a further 40% tax on their estate on their death is iniquitous. The problems are that too few people really have a long-term plan for mitigating inheritance tax, and too few people can afford to make significantly large gifts of capital.

Business Property Relief, on the other hand, is attractive because it can speed up the process of getting IHT exemption. Furthermore, it doesn't require you to give up ownership or control of the money. But investments of this nature need to be approached with a degree of caution. To understand why I'll first briefly explain how Business Property Relief came about.

Business Property Relief was introduced in 1976 with the original intention of enabling family businesses to be passed down through generations without incurring an inheritance tax liability.

Business Property Relief is no longer restricted to family businesses. Qualifying investments now include other UK businesses not quoted on the Stock Market, along with some businesses quoted on the Alternative Investment Market (AIM) – though not every industry or activity listed on AIM is qualifying.

So, rather than having to gift money away, and then waiting a full seven years for IHT exemption, qualifying Business Property Relief investments benefit from 100% IHT relief after just two years. And you retain ownership and control of the capital.

But investments into unquoted or AIM listed shares, carry higher risk and volatility than investments in larger listed companies. This can be a problem if life expectancy is relatively short, and where there is high risk that markets will fall.

As attractive as these schemes are, they tend to work better the longer they have been running. Over the longer term, short term blips in the market will even themselves out, whereas if you've left the planning to the last minute, market falls could be as damaging as the tax you're trying to save.

I suppose that what I'm trying to say is this; inheritance tax planning is something couples should discuss together, rather than being a last minute short-term fix. Whereas the short-term last minute fix is something that I often see happening, as the surviving spouse looks for ways to reduce the potential inheritance tax liability.

Investments in unlisted and AIM shares work best the longer they are held, as time tends to reduce the effects of volatility.

Summary

Businesses can bring a lot of complexity on death, but they can also create opportunity. The opportunity is business assets being treated favourably for inheritance tax purposes. The problem is that you may leave behind an ownership problem, particularly with smaller or family owned businesses.

If there is a lot of personal wealth tied up in the business there should be a means of protecting and/or extracting that wealth in the event of death. This is where life insurance can be very beneficial, as it ensures there is money in the hands of the right people, at the right time. But equally, it is important to take appropriate advice from people who understand the problems, and who have the experience to provide the right solution.

If you are in business you should ask yourself the following questions:

- What will happen to my business on my death?
- Who do I want my business to pass to?
- Does the business have a value if I die?
- How easy would it be for my beneficiaries to sell my business?
- Do I need to consider a trust to keep business assets out of my beneficiary's estate?
- How would other shareholders or partners purchase my shares from my spouse?
- What is the business succession plan?

- Do my professional advisers know what they are?
- Do my shareholders and partners know what they are?

For many people, understanding what will happen to their business, and making financial plans to deal with the circumstances after their death, involves first acknowledging the problems exist. But just as with making a will, people who carry out good business succession planning will undoubtedly have greater peace of mind that their inheritance will go where they intended it to go.

Similarly, couples embarking on inheritance tax planning early will be in greater control of the outcome than a surviving spouse who feels that time is running out. Business property relief is a good inheritance tax planning tool, but becomes all the more effective, the earlier it is deployed.

Chapter Eleven
The Trusted Team

WHEN I STARTED making notes about the "trusted team" I remembered something widely attributed to Michael Winner (the movie director who has since passed away). He is believed to have said; "teamwork is a lot of people doing what I say". Most likely it was said 'tongue in cheek' but perhaps there was an element of truth to it.

I say that because there has been a lot of press comment about his estate since his death. It seems there isn't enough money to go round. His widow, Geraldine, was quoted in the Times newspaper as complaining that she doesn't have enough money to live on because 'they' have frozen his bank accounts. She doesn't elaborate on who 'they' are - though we might assume she means the banks and the solicitors dealing with his estate.

The solicitors quite correctly notified the banks of his death (though the banks probably heard it first from the news reports). In turn, the banks will have frozen the accounts until they receive instructions from whoever is granted probate.

This is standard procedure and ensures the assets remain in the estate to pay any outstanding liabilities such as income and inheritance tax. Equally, they shouldn't release any money without knowing who it actually belongs to.

So what could they have done? Where a couple's expenditure is largely met by one of them (and we'll assume it's the husband), and bank accounts are in that person's sole name, it is important the spouse has sufficient money in her name to pay bills and living expenses. At the very least there should be a readily accessible emergency fund.

It could easily be several months before the estate is finally sorted; quite a long time to be without any money. A simple way of dealing with this is to hold one or more bank accounts in joint names. Then, on production of the death certificate any accounts in joint names will automatically pass to the surviving account holder.

But if being locked out of her late husband's bank accounts wasn't bad enough, the Daily Mail subsequently reported that she's unlikely to receive what he supposedly left her. The same goes for the other beneficiaries named in his Will.

Apart from his widow, Winner left his long time personal assistant £300,000 and a £1.2 million flat. He also left £600,000 and another flat to a former mistress, and supposedly a further £1 million to another lady friend. This is on top of the £5 million he left his wife. Any residue from the estate goes to the charity he founded - the Police Memorial Trust.

The problem is; although the estate was initially valued at £16.8 million it shrinks to £4.75 million after his debts are paid. That doesn't even cover the £5 million left to his wife, never mind any gifts to other beneficiaries.

Even the flats have mortgages secured on them. His personal assistant, who has been occupying the flat for some time, has been asked to stump up £150,000 inheritance tax, and to repay the £600,000 mortgage. She says she doesn't have the money.

Yet many of these problems could have been avoided had Michael Winner worked with a 'trusted team' rather than individual advisers.

It's hard to imagine a team of professional advisers not alerting Winner to any potential problems if they'd been aware of all the facts. My conclusion is he chose not to share everything with his advisers.

If there had been a 'trusted team' of advisers they would have highlighted the consequences of gifting property with a loan secured against it. I don't think for a moment that Michael Winner expected to leave his long-term assistant with a £150,000 inheritance tax bill and a £600,000 mortgage, but that's what she's got.

Had his lawyers been aware of insufficient assets in the estate to meet his bequests they would have told him the assets would most likely be sold, and his bequests apportioned on a pro-rata basis, including those due to his wife.

Each of the beneficiaries has appointed probate solicitors to pursue their inheritances. They will incur additional cost that none of them want, or can easily afford.

Your affairs may not be as complicated as Winner's estate, and the sums involved may be different, but that doesn't mean problems can't arise. Having a trusted team working with you means problems can be anticipated, and solutions found in good time.

So who do you select for your team of trusted advisers?

For most families with a reasonable level of assets the team is likely to include their financial adviser/planner, their solicitor and their accountant. Where there are fewer assets it may be the financial adviser/planner is the main point of contact and advice. The team may also include family members who may have been appointed as executors of the estate, or to become guardians of any young children, or act as trustees where necessary.

Let's consider briefly what each of the main professions can add to the 'trusted team', and how they can work together effectively to ensure your estate is able to cope following your death, and your dependants can continue to function without unnecessary financial worry.

The Financial Planner

I'll begin with the subject I know most about - the role of the financial planner. The role has evolved beyond all recognition from the early days of financial advice. Twenty-five years ago, when I began, financial advice was very much a transactional process. Advisers were chiefly selling financial products such as pensions, savings plans, and collective investments like unit trusts and insurance company funds.

What a financial planner does today is far more relational and involves mainly planning, guidance, and some coaching. Also, it's not unusual for me to have regular contact with clients throughout the year. We aim to ensure they remain 'on track' through following the plans they established.

Sometimes we'll adapt their plans to take account of any changes that may arise. They could be changes to tax rates, interest rates and the economy in general, or it could be personal circumstances changing to do with their job, unexpected windfalls, or occasionally bereavement.

When working with a new client we first establish what's most important to them, typically expressed as their goals, and their values around those goals. Some of these goals will be 'must haves' whilst others are 'nice to have' and thus less important. It's important to establish which ones are which.

It may be that achieving financial independence by a particular age is a 'must have' (financial independence doesn't necessarily mean retirement, but being able to choose whether you continue working or not) whereas a second home/holiday home is a 'nice to have'.

We'll then agree what the cost of reaching the 'must have' goals is likely to be, taking into account inflation. That essentially becomes their number,[1] the amount of money required to achieve their goals and live their lives with some financial stability.

Once someone knows what their number is (and so few people do know what their target number is) we can calculate whether they are on track to achieve it, or how far off they might be. Armed with that information it is possible to structure a plan to get someone on track and then keep on track. Not only that, but by setting goals that you own, and seeing how the plan can get you there, tends to help people stick to the plan.

Of course, the plan is not a blue-print to be followed slavishly; circumstances change, goals shift, and the financial landscape changes. But by regularly reviewing goals and plans with you, we can suggest appropriate adjustments along the way.

---

1   Please see The Number by Lee Eisenberg - a book review on page 169

From time to time throughout the relationship we'll need the input from other professionals, typically lawyers and accountants. Anticipating any potential legal problems can make the difference between a successful plan and an unsuccessful one.

Likewise, the accountant can help ensure that we're not unwittingly walking into a tax problem, or can show how doing something a different way can be more tax efficient.

So let's take a look at how we might use a lawyer.

The Lawyer

At various stages in our life most of us will use a Lawyer. Whether it's to buy or sell property, arrange a Will, or to assist in divorce, we engage lawyers to help with the legal aspects of our lives.

And as we get older we tend to use lawyers more – perhaps to establish a family trust, arrange a Lasting Power of Attorney, or to act as executors of our estate. Lawyers can help with all of these issues and more, but it is important to choose the right lawyer for the job, and the right lawyer for you.

But if you don't already have a relationship with a lawyer, finding the right one may feel a little daunting. After all, we tend only to approach them at stressful times of our lives, buying a property for example, and it can also feel very transactional rather than relational.

Even if we do have a family lawyer relationship, we tend not to have regular contact with them in the same way we might with an accountant or our financial planner/adviser. Yet in my role I find having regular contact with lawyers is beneficial to the work I do with my clients.

When I'm in contact with a client's other professional advisers I can informally run ideas past them (and vice versa) before working up a proposal to put forward to the client. If something won't work for whatever reason, then we haven't incurred costs for our clients unnecessarily. And by working together, we're often able to make cost savings because we're able to share information quickly.

So, how do you find a good lawyer, one that you feel able to ask questions, can provide the services that you require, and one you can afford? Often your other advisers can recommend someone but even so, it is helpful to have a basis on which to choose.

First of all, what do you need a lawyer for? Legal services can be complex so you need to find one with the right level of experience for the issue you have. Someone who has been doing your conveyancing, may be unsuitable when it comes to drafting complex Wills and Trusts for example.

You also need to appoint a lawyer who you can work with - this is as much a personality decision as anything else, but you need to feel comfortable enough asking questions, no matter how stupid they may seem to you. If you don't feel able to then perhaps you've got the wrong lawyer. Most that I have worked with are very approachable, and care a great deal about their clients, and the outcomes they want to achieve.

Be aware it will be a two way process. When arranging a Will or a Lasting Power of Attorney, your lawyer will ask a lot of personal questions about you, your possessions and the people you're connected to. Whilst your lawyer can offer advice about bequests, or who should act as your Attorney, ultimately these decisions are yours.

So think clearly about the outcomes you are looking for. In fact the clearer you are, and the less you need to go back and forth, the lower your costs are going to be. If you know what you want, your lawyer can estimate the costs and is more likely to be on budget than if there are numerous revisions along the way.

Costs are an important factor, and you should understand how your lawyer charges for advice. Is it based on an hourly rate, or a fixed fee? Some will charge a percentage of the estate if they're acting as executors. Don't be afraid to ask how they charge, and ask them to explain it in detail if you don't understand.

Ask what would happen if the work they're undertaking turns out to be more complex than first thought. If they charge hourly, ask for an estimate of how many hours the work will take. No one likes a nasty surprise, least of all a higher than expected legal bill.

You also want to know how they expect to take instructions from you, and how they will keep you informed of progress. Does everything need to be done face to face, for example, or can it be done by email and telephone? This has time and cost implications. Are they happy to work alongside your other advisers?

Will they put all their advice in writing so that you can read it in your own time before making a decision? Do you know how do you like to receive information, what about your spouse? And how quickly are you able to make decision? Does your spouse like making financial or legal decisions? This is an important consideration if there'll be a need for ongoing help and advice post bereavement. It needs to be a professional relationship that all parties are comfortable with.

I suppose what I'm saying is; building a good relationship with a lawyer, and one where there is ongoing contact, will help prevent problems arising at the wrong time i.e. when there's nothing that can be done.

The Accountant

Accountants come in all shapes and sizes; for example, if you're a company owner you may need an accountant with specific corporate experience or auditing skills, whereas an individual may only want someone to complete their annual personal tax return.

People with complex tax arrangements, or a significant level of wealth, may find it preferable to work closely with an accountant. Not only does this ensure the annual 'tax compliance' work is completed and submitted on time, but an experienced tax specialist will usually be a good sounding board to discuss any tax planning solutions.

For people of even modest means, the cost of an accountant for annual tax compliance work is unlikely to be overly expensive, and it frees up time that can be spent doing less tiresome things. Furthermore, they usually manage to pick up on tax savings issues that might otherwise be ignored.

I regularly meet people who have failed to claim all their tax allowances and tax reliefs. Things like higher rate relief on pension contributions and charity donations seem to be common omissions. Claiming these can mean the accountant's bill is largely covered through the tax savings they make.

I've also noticed that as people become older they're less inclined to want to deal with this themselves, and are happy to hand responsibility to someone else. Tax affairs ceased being simple a long time ago and now it's harder to get help and advice from your local tax office. An accountant is becoming more of a necessity than a luxury!

From the perspective of a trusted team, the accountant can play an important part following bereavement. If you've had a long-term relationship with an accountant they will have historic records of things like gifts made, any trust related transactions, and investment transactions. With this information they will be able to assist with providing accurate information to the probate office following bereavement

They will also be able to advise on the effectiveness of any schemes you may wish to consider as part of any inheritance tax planning. Particularly when looking at family business issues and the aspect of Business Property Relief for example.

Summary

A trusted team is a valuable resource during your lifetime, and the longer you work with them, and the longer they are able to work alongside each other on your behalf, the more likely they will understand your needs and concerns. They will also be the people your dependants can turn to in a time of crisis, so that where there is a danger of costly mistakes arising, they can be avoided.

I realise that some people see advisers as an expense rather than an asset, but a good team can have a positive influence on individual wealth and quality of life. There has been some recent research done by Morningstar (the fund management analysts) who have been able to quantify the added value that advisers bring through helping people make better decisions. In a nutshell, investors using advisers tended to achieve better long-term results than those who don't work with advisers.

Part Two

Part Two

Chapter Twelve
Types of Insurance

WE READILY BUY insurance to cover against the loss or damage to our valuable assets. Sometimes insurance cover is compulsory, like car insurance covering damage to third parties, or a mortgage lender insisting on insurance to cover the cost of rebuilding the property.

However, we often fail to insure the one thing we (or our dependants) depend on most, our life. When someone is dependent upon another person being alive or in good health, surely it makes sense to insure against that person dying or being incapacitated?

But what type of insurance should you buy? The following is a brief guide to the simple life insurance contracts available today. It doesn't include anything more complicated than simple protection policies - if your needs are more complex it is worth taking professional advice.

Let's begin with the simplest form of life insurance policy.

Temporary life insurance
(also called term assurance)

This type of policy provides insurance cover at a fixed price (called the premium) for a specific period of time (the term). Temporary insurance is usually the least expensive way of purchasing a large sum assured (the amount payable on death) for a given premium over a specific period of time.

Once the term expires then cover ceases. Some policies may include the option to purchase further insurance, though the premium will almost certainly increase. Many policies having the option to buy a new policy, will usually allow you to extend cover without any further medical underwriting - this means that you would be able to extend cover regardless of your state of health.

If the insured person dies during the term, the death benefit will be paid to whoever is entitled to the money according to the terms of the contract - this person is called the beneficiary.

Temporary assurance is one of the earliest types of life insurance, and also one of the simplest, though there are variants that allow it to be tailored to specific needs. It is most often used to provide a single capital sum on the death, though some policies will pay a guaranteed annual amount for a specific number of years.

The contract terms are simple; term assurance promises to pay the sum assured, on the death of the life assured, provided all premiums are paid up to date, and the policy has not expired. It does not have a saving or investment element, and there is no return of premiums if the policy is not claimed against. The policy can be cancelled before the end of the term, though there is no refund of premiums, and cover will cease.

What does it cover?

Because temporary life insurance provides pure death benefits, it is primarily used to provide cover against financial risk for the insured or his/her beneficiaries. Risks that may need protecting include things like debt (a mortgage for example), dependant's care needs, and education costs (school or university fees).

Most of these risks are not permanent and thus "Whole of Life" insurance policies are not generally needed in these situations. Providing permanent insurance protection over a person's lifetime is considerably more expensive as there will be a claim in the future, everyone dies eventually.

Ordinarily, providing financial protection for a spouse is often only needed until retirement, which is the point that retirement savings kick-in to provide the required financial security. Besides, the costs of the premiums may become prohibitive with older age.

Level term life insurance

The most common form of temporary insurance is guaranteed, level premium, term insurance. These policies have a premium that is guaranteed to remain the same for a given period of years. The term selected can range from as low as one year, to over thirty years depending on your requirements. For example, many people will have a twenty-five year term insurance running alongside a twenty-five year mortgage.

The premium paid each year remains the same for the duration of the contract. However, the insurer will base their costs on the aggregate cost of the annual renewable term rates. The longer the term, the higher the premium will be, this is because the older you become, the more expensive the insurance is. The more expensive later year's premiums are averaged into the annual premium. You effectively pay more in the earlier years, but less in the later years.

Most level term insurance providers will offer a renewal option, allowing the insurance to be renewed for a further guaranteed period, if the term needs to be extended. This option increases the cost of the premium. Not every policy has this option, nor does every policy have guaranteed insurability. Individual policy conditions should be reviewed carefully to ensure they meet your needs.

Some policies also include an option to convert the term policy to a Whole Life policy. This option can be useful to a person who purchased the term life policy whilst in good health, and is later diagnosed with a condition that makes it difficult to obtain a new policy.

Again, specific policy conditions should be reviewed carefully to see whether there are any time limits or exclusions. For anyone diagnosed with a terminal illness this can be a useful feature, especially when considering the financial security of dependants.

Some term insurance policies also have a feature whereby the sum assured is paid out early in the event the insured person is diagnosed with a terminal illness. This may provide a welcome capital sum to assist with care, or any other arrangements.

Decreasing Term Assurance

Decreasing Term Assurance is where the amount of cover reduces over the term. When used alongside a repayment mortgage, the sum assured reduces as the outstanding mortgage reduces. This keeps premiums lower then if the sum assured remained static throughout the term.

Family Income Benefit

For young families this type of insurance offers great benefits and value. Family Income Benefit allows you to purchase a very high initial level of cover, for a relatively low premium compared to level term insurance.

If your family needed £50,000 to live on if you died, and they needed this amount for the next 20 years, the ideal policy would pay £50,000 each year to your dependants. The further you are into the term before the benefits are payable, the lower the amount of cover that is needed.

The alternative is a 20-year level term policy with a £1million sum assured. This would pay £1million whether you died in year one or in the final year of cover. However, the costs of providing £1million of cover in the final year is significantly more expensive than providing the £50,000 that is actually needed.

Family Income Benefit assurance is a form of decreasing term insurance, and the sum assured reduces each year, meaning that as the risk reduces, the cover reduces. This keeps the premium low. Family Income Benefit therefore provides a very high level of cover at the outset, but at a much lower premium than under a comparable level term assurance.

How long should the term be?

The term selected depends on your personal circumstances, and this can be down to two factors – dependants and debts. Two of the biggest triggers for taking out an insurance policy are; starting a family and taking out a mortgage.

How much life cover do I need?

First find out whether you already have life insurance through your employer. Many firms offer a death in service benefit that will pay out if you die while still working for the company. This is typically between two and four times your salary. Then ask yourself whether this is enough.

Next, look at the size of your debts, how much you earn, and the financial needs of your dependants. There should be sufficient insurance cover to enable them to maintain an acceptable lifestyle if you were not there to support them.

The more debt, and the more expenses you have, the higher the amount of insurance you need to buy. Of course, the more insurance you have the higher the premiums will be.

How much will it cost?

There are three other factors insurers take into account when working out the premium – your age, your health and your occupation. All three will influence your life expectancy, and therefore have a bearing on the cost.

Those who are older when they take out life insurance will pay more as their life expectancy is shorter. This also applies to people in poor health, or those who have had a serious medical condition in the past. Or where there is a family history of things like heart problems. Finally, people whose job involves more risk will also pay higher premiums. For example, an office worker will pay less than a deep-sea diver.

You must tell your insurer if you have ever suffered a serious illness, or are currently receiving treatment when you apply for life cover. If you don't and the insurer finds out after your death, the company is likely to refuse to pay out.

Some policies have reviewable premiums. With these policies the premium will be reviewed after a period of time, typically after 10 years, and then more frequently thereafter. At the review the premiums could go up. Guaranteed premiums are more expensive at the outset, but usually offer better value in the long run as the premiums will remain the same throughout the term of the policy.

Joint or single life?

It's natural to assume that it's better to take out a joint policy, but this might not be the best thing to do. A joint policy is not necessarily significantly cheaper than two separate single life policies. Furthermore, a joint policy will only pay out once on the first death, leaving the second person without cover. If they then needed to buy additional cover it will be more costly for them because they will be older.

Buying two single life policies also provides additional flexibility. It allows you to insure yourselves for different amounts, and for different lengths of time.

Put your life insurance policy in trust

It is simple case to ask your life insurer to write your policy in a trust when you take it out. The insurer will often handle all the paperwork for you. The reason for this is that the money intended for your beneficiaries will not be added to your estate if it's in a trust, so the payout won't be liable for inheritance tax (IHT) if your assets are over the IHT threshold.

By by putting your life insurance in trust, it avoids it being added to the value of your estate for IHT purposes, and your family will receive the money quicker, as it doesn't have to go through probate, (the legal process by which your estate is valued and distributed according to your will).

Chapter Thirteen
Wills and Probate

IN PART ONE I outlined the importance of making a Will. Before looking at the process in more detail it is worth reviewing some of the reasons why it is important:-

- If you die without a valid will, there are certain rules which dictate how your estate (your money, property and possessions) should be allocated. This may different to the way you want your estate distributed.

- Unmarried partners and those not in registered a civil partnership will not automatically inherit from each other unless there is a Will. In these situations the death of one partner may create serious financial issues for the surviving partner.

- You need to make a will detailing the arrangements for any children you may have, should one or both parents die.

- It may be possible to reduce the amount of inheritance tax payable by your estate. Not having a Will does not allow you to plan effectively.

- If your circumstances have changed, for example you have separated, divorced or married/remarried (or entered into a civil partnership), it is important that you make a will to ensure that your money and possessions are distributed according to your wishes.

Rules of Intestacy

When a person dies without leaving a valid will, their estate will be shared out according to certain rules. These are called the rules of intestacy, and a person who dies without leaving a will is called an intestate person. Even if someone has a Will, but it is not legally valid, the rules of intestacy will determine how the estate is divided.

The only people who can inherit under the rules of intestacy are married or civil partners, and some other close relatives.

Married and civil partners

Partners can only inherit under the rules of intestacy if they are actually married or in a civil partnership at the time of death. If you are divorced or if your civil partnership has been legally ended, you can't inherit under the rules of intestacy. However, partners who have separated informally can still inherit under the rules of intestacy.

If there are any surviving children, grandchildren or great grandchildren of the person who died, and if the estate is valued greater than £250,000, the surviving partner will inherit:

- All personal property and belongings of the deceased and
- the first £250,000 of the estate, and
- a life interest in half of the remaining estate.
- A life interest means that you cannot dispose of or spend that part of the estate.
- You do, however, have the benefit of it during your lifetime.

If the estate is worth more than £450,000, and there are no surviving children, grandchildren or great-grandchildren, but there are surviving parents, the partner will inherit:

- All personal property and belongings of the deceased and
- the first £450,000 of the estate (plus interest from the date of death) and
- one-half of the remaining estate.

If the estate is worth more than £450,000, but there are no surviving children, grandchildren, great-grandchildren or parents, yet there are surviving brothers, sisters, nephews or nieces, the partner will inherit:

- All personal property and belongings of the deceased and
- the first £450,000 of the estate with interest from the date of death and
- one-half of the remaining estate.

Jointly-owned Property

Many couples jointly own their home, and there are two different ways of jointly owning a home. These are known as joint tenancies and tenancies in common.

If the couple were joint tenants at the time of the death, the surviving partner will automatically inherit the other partner's share of the property. However, if they were tenants in common, the surviving partner does not automatically inherit the other person's share.

Couples may also have joint bank or building society accounts. If one dies, the other partner will automatically inherit the whole of the money.

Any jointly held property and money that the surviving partner inherits will not count as part of the estate of the person who has died under the intestacy rules.

Children

As outlined earlier, children of the intestate person will inherit only if the estate is worth more than a certain amount. However, if there is no surviving married or civil partner, the children of the deceased will inherit the whole estate. This applies regardless of how much the estate is worth. If there are two or more children, the estate will be divided equally between them.

Children - if there is a surviving partner

If there is a surviving partner, a child only inherits from the estate if the estate is valued greater than £250,000. Again, if there are two or more children, they will inherit the following in equal shares:-

- One half of the value of the estate above £250,000 and

- the other half of the value of the estate above £250,000 when the surviving partner dies.

All the children of the parent who has died intestate will inherit equally from the estate. This applies where a parent has children from different relationships, even if the child's parents were not married or in a registered civil partnership. The rules also apply to adopted children, and adopted stepchildren.

Children do not receive their inheritance immediately. They receive it when they:

- Reach the age of 18, or
- marry or form a civil partnership under this age.

Until then, the money is held in trust, with trustees managing the inheritance on their behalf.

Grandchildren and great grandchildren

A grandchild or great grandchild will inherit from the estate of an intestate person only if:

- Their parent or grandparent has died before the intestate person, or
- their parent is alive when the intestate person dies, but subsequently dies before reaching the age of 18 without having married or forming a civil partnership

In these circumstances, the grandchildren and great grandchildren will inherit equal shares of the share which their parent or grandparent would have been entitled.

Other close relatives

Parents, brothers and sisters and nieces and nephews of the intestate person may inherit under the rules of intestacy. This will depend on a number of circumstances:

- Whether there is a surviving married or civil partner.
- Whether there are children, grandchildren or great grandchildren.
- In the case of nephews and nieces, whether the parent directly related to the person who has died is also dead.
- The value of the estate.

Other relatives may also have a right to inherit if the person who died intestate had no surviving married or civil partner, or any children, grandchildren, great grand-children, parents, brothers, sisters, nephews or nieces. The order of priority amongst other relatives is as follows:-

- Grandparents.
- Uncles and aunts. A cousin can inherit instead if the uncle or aunt who would have inherited died before the intestate person.
- Half-uncles and half-aunts. A half-cousin can inherit instead, if the half-uncle or half-aunt who would have inherited, died before the intestate person.

If there are no surviving relatives

If there are no surviving relatives who can inherit under the rules of intestacy, the estate passes to the Crown. The Treasury Solicitor is then responsible for dealing with the estate. The Crown can make grants from the estate but does not have to agree to them.

If you are not a surviving relative, but you believe you have a good reason to apply for a grant, for example, you had been financially dependent on the deceased you should seek legal advice.

Rearranging the way the estate is distributed

It is possible to rearrange the way property is distributed when someone dies intestate, provided this is done within two years of their death. This is called making a deed of family arrangement or variation. All the people who would inherit under the rules of intestacy must agree.

If they agree, the property can be shared out in a different way so that people who do not inherit under the intestacy rules can still get some of the estate. Or they could agree that the amount that people get is different to the amount they would get under the rules of intestacy.

Applying for financial help

If you were living with the deceased, but you were not married or in a civil partnership, you would not inherit under the rules of intestacy. However, you could apply to court for financial help. To apply you must have lived together for at least two years immediately before their death. You must apply within a certain time limit although this can be extended in certain circumstances.

The court may order:

- Regular payments from the estate.
- A lump sum payment from the estate.
- Property to be transferred from the estate.

Making a Will

When drawing up a Will it is easy to make mistakes, and these may invalidate the Will leading to the deceased being deemed intestate.

Some common mistakes when making a Will are:-

- Not being aware of the formal requirements needed to make a Will legally valid.

- Not taking into account all of the money and property available in the estate.

- Failing to deal with the possibility that a beneficiary may predecease the person making the Will.

- Making changes to the Will and not making sure the alterations are signed and witnessed, thus making them invalid.

- Not being aware of the effect of marriage, a registered civil partnership, divorce or dissolution of a civil partnership.

- Not making suitable provision for dependants. They can claim from the estate if they believe they are not adequately provided for.

When making a Will it is not necessary for it to be drawn up or witnessed by a solicitor. If you want to make a Will yourself you can - there are even ready-made templates that can be purchased from good quality stationers or online. But for anything other than the most straightforward Will, professional advice is recommended. Sorting out disputes and misunderstandings after your death is likely to result in considerable legal costs, thus reducing the amount of money in the estate.

When to use a solicitor

For more complex situations it is advisable to use a solicitor. Examples I have previously encountered include:-

- Making provision for a dependant who is unable to care for themselves, particular instances include disabled children whose long term care needs careful consideration.

- Where there are nationality and residency issues, or where your main home is overseas.

- Where there are overseas assets, such as property.

- You own property with someone who is not your husband, wife or civil partner.

- There are business interests involved.

Things to consider before seeing a solicitor

To save time and reduce costs when using solicitor, you should give some thought to what you want included in your will. You should consider things like:-

- What assets you have. Make a list of all your chattels, property, savings, occupational and personal pensions, insurance policies, shares and other investments.

- Make a list of all the people that you wish to receive money or possessions. These people are known as beneficiaries. Who should benefit if your beneficiaries should die before you. Consider whether you wish to leave any money to charity.

- Who would look after any children under 18.
- Who will act as your executors? These are the people who will sort out the estate and carry out your wishes as set out in the Will.

Executors

Executors are responsible for carrying out your wishes and for sorting out your estate. They have to collect together all the assets of the estate, and deal with all the paperwork. They pay all the debts, taxes, funeral and administration costs out of money in the estate. They also make gifts and transfer property to your beneficiaries.

You do not need to appoint more than one executor, though if one of them dies it might be advisable to have named another. Typically there are two executors appointed. The people most commonly appointed are:-

- Relatives or friends.
- Solicitors or accountants.
- Banks.
- In England and Wales, the Public Trustee or in some cases the Official Solicitor if there is no one else willing and able to act.

Choose your executors carefully since their job involves a considerable amount of work and responsibility. You should ask the person you are thinking of appointing as an executor to see if they will agree to take on the responsibility. Even if they initially agree and are subsequently appointed, they have a right to refuse if they are no longer willing to act.

The Requirements for a Valid Will

For a will to be valid, the person making it must be:-

- Aged 18 years old or over; and
- made voluntarily; and
- made by a person who is of sound mind; and
- be in writing; and
- signed by the person making the Will in the presence of two witnesses; and
- signed by the two witnesses, in the presence of the person making the Will, after it has been signed.
- A witness, or the married partner of a witness, cannot benefit from the Will. If a
- witness is a beneficiary (or the married partner or civil partner of a beneficiary),
- the Will remains valid but the beneficiary is unable to inherit under the Will.

Although a Will can be legally valid even if it is not dated, it is preferable to ensure that the will includes the date on which it is signed. This is particularly useful if there are several versions of a person's Will. The most recent is the one that counts.

The Will is only complete once it is signed and witnessed properly.

Safekeeping of a will

Once made, the Will should be kept in a safe place. It is important that no other documents are attached to it. There are a several places where you can keep a Will:-

- The most obvious is at home; or
- with a solicitor or accountant; or
- at a bank in their safe deposit storage.

It is also possible to store it at the Principal Registry of the Family Division of the High Court, a District Registry or Probate Sub-Registry for safe-keeping. If you wish to deposit a Will in this way you should visit the District Registry or Probate Sub-Registry or write to:-

The Probate Department,

The Principal Registry of the Family Division,

First Avenue House,

42-49 High Holborn,

London

WC1V 6NP

In Northern Ireland, wills can be deposited with:-

Probate Office

Royal Courts of Justice

Chichester Street

Belfast

BT1 3JF

Locating a Will after someone dies

When someone close to you has died, and you think they made a Will but you can't find one, there are several things you can try in order to locate it. First, check to see if you can find a certificate of deposit - it will have been sent to them if they arranged for the will to be kept by the Principal Registry of the Family Division.

Even if you can't find a certificate of deposit, you should still check with the Registry to see if they hold the Will. If the person died in a residential or nursing home you should check to see if the Will was left with them. You should also contact the person's solicitor, accountant, financial adviser, or their bank to see if they hold the Will.

If you can't find a Will, you will usually have to deal with the deceased's estate as if they died without leaving a Will.

Making Changes to a Will

After a Will has been made, it is important to keep it up to date to take account of changes in circumstances. Many people will make a Will and then not review it for several years, or even decades! It is recommended you review the contents of a Will regularly to make sure it still reflects your wishes. Common changes of circumstances which affect a Will are:-

- Marriage, remarriage or registering a civil partnership.
- Divorce, or dissolving a civil partnership, or separating.
- The birth or adoption of children.

Changing your Will due to a change of circumstances should not be done by amending the original after it has been signed and witnessed. Any obvious alterations are assumed to have been made later, and would not form part of the original legally valid Will.

The only way you can change a Will is by making:-

- A codicil to the Will; or
- a new Will.

Codicils

A codicil is a supplement to a Will, which makes some alterations but leaves the rest of it intact. This might be done, for example, to increase a legacy, or to add beneficiaries.

A codicil must be signed by the same person who made the original Will. It must then be witnessed in the same way. The witnesses do not have to be the same as for the original Will.

There is no limit on the number of codicils can be added to a Will, however, if a complicated change is involved, it is advisable to make a new Will.

Making a New Will

If you wish to make major changes to a Will, it is advisable to make a new one. The new Will should begin with a clause stating that it revokes all previous Wills and codicils. The old/previous Will should be destroyed. Revoking a Will means that it is no longer legally valid.

Probate & Dealing with the Deceased's Estate

All the assets owned by the deceased is known as their estate. The estate may comprise of:

- Money, held in cash or in a bank or building society account. It may also include money paid out on a life insurance policy.
- Money owed to the deceased.
- Stocks, shares and other investments.
- Property, for example, their home, holiday homes, rental property.
- Personal possessions and chattels.

If the deceased owes money to other people, for example, on a credit card, or a mortgage, this comes out of the estate.

The person who deals with the estate of the deceased is called the executor or an administrator. The executor will be someone named in the Will as responsible for dealing with the estate. Even so, they may have to apply for a legal authority before they can deal with the estate. This is called probate.

On the other hand, an administrator is someone who is responsible for dealing with an estate under certain circumstances, such as where there is no Will or the named executors are unwilling to act. An administrator has to apply for letters of administration before they can deal with an estate.

It is usually against the law to start sharing out the estate, or to get money from the estate, until probate or letters of administration have been issued. However, you do not always need letters of administration to be able to deal with the estate of someone who has died, though you Will usually need probate or letters of administration if the estate includes property. You may not need probate or letters of administration if:

- The estate is just made up of cash and personal possessions.
- All the property in the estate is owned as joint tenants; it automatically becomes wholly owned by the other owner.
- The amount of money is small.
- The estate is insolvent and there is insufficient money in the estate to pay all the debts, taxes and expenses.

The time it takes to get probate or letters of administration will vary according to the circumstances. It may only take a few weeks if there are no complications and the estate is straightforward. If inheritance tax is due, the forms are filled in incorrectly, or it is a complicated estate, then it may take longer. It could take years in the most complicated cases.

To apply for probate or letters of administration, you need to complete several forms. You will always need to fill in form PA1. This asks for details about the deceased, their surviving relatives, the personal representative and some details about the Will. Other forms may be required depending on what is in the estate and how much it is worth.

You can get an application pack from any local probate registry or by telephoning the HMRC Probate and Inheritance Tax Helpline. The forms and leaflets are also available on the internet. PA1 can be found at www.gov.uk and other forms are available from HMRC website at www.hmrc.gov.uk

When you have sent in the forms you will be asked to go for an interview at a probate registry, so return the forms to the probate registry where you would like to go for the interview. You also have to send:

- The original Will (if there is one).
- The death certificate.
- The probate fee.

Make sure you keep copies of the forms you have filled in.

The fee for applying for probate or letters of administration depends on the value of the estate. There is no fee where the value of the estate is less than £5,000. The fee for an estate valued at £5,000 or more is £105.

When they have received and looked at your forms, the probate registry will contact you to go for an interview at the probate registry. You will be asked to take all relevant documents and letters with you, such as bank statements and share certificates. You also need to take identification with you, for example, your passport or driving licence.

At the time of the interview the probate registry will have completed the official legal papers with all the details you have previously provided. You should check all the details carefully as you are legally responsible for making sure the documents are correct.

Whether Probate or Letters of Administration is needed or not, the executor or administrator will be responsible for dealing with all of the estate, including:-

- Locating all financial documentation belonging to the deceased.

- Sending a copy of the death certificate to all organisations that hold the money of the deceased.

- Obtain confirmation of the value of the money at the date of death, and the amount of income received during the last tax year up to the date of death.

- Request that bank accounts are frozen so no one can take money out without the correct legal authority.

- Opening a bank account on behalf of the estate to collect all money owed to the estate from banks, pension funds, insurance policies etc.

- Obtaining any other money owed to the estate.

- Finding out if the deceased owed any money, and paying any debts, expenses and fees.

- Listing details of the property, money and possessions and debts in the estate.

- Calculating the amount of inheritance tax due and arranging to pay it.

- Dealing with the documents required by the probate registry and HM Revenue and Customs.

- Distributing the estate, in accordance with the Will or the rules of intestacy.

If there are insufficient assets in the estate to cover the outstanding tax, expenses, bills and other liabilities, you should seek the advice of a solicitor.

Tax and benefits

It is important to sort out a deceased person's benefits, tax and National Insurance as soon as possible. There may still be some income tax to pay or their estate may receive a tax rebate. You should tell the tax office, and the benefits office about the death.

Chapter Fourteen
Power of Attorney

THERE ARE TWO types of Power of Attorney: these are called Ordinary and Lasting. If you want someone to be able to make decisions and take action concerning your finances while you still have mental capacity, you can set up an Ordinary Power of Attorney.

This is a legal document and gives someone else (the attorney) authority to act on your (the donor) behalf. It is only valid while the donor still has mental capacity to make their own decisions about their finances. This ensures they can keep an eye on what their attorney is doing.

You can limit the power you give to your attorney so that they can only deal with certain assets. For example you may restrict the authority to a single bank account, or it could extend to all your accounts as well as your home.

If you no longer have mental capacity the Ordinary Power of Attorney is no longer valid. In these situations a Lasting Power of Attorney is required.

As long as you have mental capacity, you can set up a Lasting Power of Attorney (LPA) to give someone the authority to make decisions on your behalf. There are two types of LPA: A Property and Financial Affairs LPA covers decisions about the donor's property and money, and a Personal Welfare LPA covers decisions about the donor's healthcare and personal welfare.

As you can imagine, the role of the attorney involves considerable responsibility, so you should think carefully about who you appoint. You must be able to trust them to make decisions that are in your best interests.

What is Mental Capacity?

Mental capacity means being able to make decisions. This includes decisions about everyday things, such as what to wear, as well as about legal issues, such as making a will. Some people may find their capacity to make decisions changes from day to day, or that they are able to make decisions about some things, but not others.

Being slow, or having difficulty understanding or communicating a decision doesn't necessarily mean a lack of mental capacity, nor does having dementia necessarily mean a person is unable to make any decisions themselves. However, there will be times when a carer, or close relative, needs to seek legal or medical advice on whether the person they are caring for has mental capacity, or whether to act under an LPA permanently.

How does someone decide?

At some point in the future, if it is decided you're unable to make your own decisions, then someone else will need to make decisions on your behalf. But before someone can make a decision on your behalf, they must have reasonable belief that you lack capacity to make a particular decision.

This could be a decision about your property and financial affairs, such as paying bills or buying things that you need. Alternatively it could be decisions about your personal welfare, such as whether you should consent to medical treatment.

Here, the words 'reasonable belief' are important because a person's capacity can change over time, or they may have capacity to make one decision but not another. If it is decided that you lack capacity, and you have someone caring for you, they will need specific authority to make some decisions on your behalf.

As mentioned earlier, for so long as you still have mental capacity, you can choose to create a Lasting Power of Attorney (LPA) to give the person this authority.

Lasting Powers of Attorney were introduced in October 2007, and replacing the old system of Enduring Powers of Attorney (EPA). However an EPA created before October 2007 still remains valid.

Two types of LPA

There are two types of LPA. One covers decisions about the donor's property and financial affairs, and is known as a Property and Financial Affairs LPA. The other covers decisions about healthcare and personal welfare, and is known as a Personal Welfare LPA.

As a donor you can specify the types of decisions the attorney can make, or alternatively you can allow the attorney to make all decisions on your behalf. You can give different attorneys different powers, one attorney may have powers under the Property and Financial Affairs LPA, whereas someone else may have powers under the Personal Welfare LPA.

Apart from the obvious differences, there is a further difference between the two types of LPA. It is possible for a Property and Financial Affairs LPA to be used while someone still has capacity, whereas a Personal Welfare LPA can only be used once the donor has lost capacity.

When setting up a Property and Finance LPA, you can also request that the attorney regularly provides you with details of income and expenditure. Once you lose mental capacity these details can also be sent to your solicitor or a family member.

Property and Financial Affairs LPA

An attorney under a Property and Financial Affairs LPA can generally make decisions on things like:

- Buying or selling a property
- Paying (or repaying) the mortgage
- Savings and investing
- Paying bills
- Providing other people access to your financial information
- Paying for repairs to property.

Personal Welfare LPA

An attorney under a Personal Welfare LPA can generally make decisions about things such as:

- Where the donor should live, including moving into a care home.

- Whether the donor should consent to medical treatment.

- Their diet.

- The people they have contact with.

- The social activities they should take part in.

When is an LPA valid?

To be valid an LPA must have been set up whilst the donor has mental capacity, and they have not been put under any undue pressure to do so. In that respect it must always be the decision of the donor.

As they are giving someone else considerable power to make decisions about their life, there must be a relationship of trust between the donor and the attorney.

To be valid, an LPA has to be signed by a certificate provider who will certify that the donor understands the LPA and was not pressurised into signing. Then the LPA must be registered with the Office of the Public Guardian. To register the LPA with the Office of the Public Guardian, you need to complete a form available from the Office of the Public Guardian, or you can download it from the gov.uk website. Alternatively, a solicitor can help you set up the LPA and register it.

There is currently a fee of £130 for registering each LPA. So to register both a Personal Welfare LPA and a Property and Financial Affairs LPA would cost £260. People on certain benefits are exempt from paying a fee. If you're on a low income but don't qualify for benefits you may be eligible for a 50 per cent discount.

The LPA must be registered while you have the mental capacity to do so. If the donor has lost mental capacity but they have signed it while they still had mental capacity, the attorney can register the LPA for them. However, during the registration process the attorney will not have power to act on the donor's behalf under the terms of the LPA.

Understanding the Role of the Attorney

Always remember that the role of attorney involves considerable power and responsibility. You should think carefully about whether there is someone you believe is able to carry out the role. When you ask that person to become your attorney, give them time to think about it, as it involves significant responsibility.

An attorney can only make decisions that you have given them authority to make. An attorney under a Property and Financial Affairs LPA, does not have authority to make decisions about your healthcare, unless they are also your attorney under a Personal Welfare LPA.

An attorney can claim back any expenses they incur when carrying out the role as your attorney. This could be postage, telephone or travel costs, for example. Their expenses can be claimed from your money, and they should keep an account of any expenses and relevant receipts. Attorneys can't claim for time spent carrying out their duties unless they are appointed as a professional attorney - such as a solicitor.

Mental Capacity Act - Principles

When someone is acting under a Lasting Power of Attorney, they must follow certain principles set out in the Mental Capacity Act. These are aimed at making sure that where you are able to make your own decisions, you should do as much as possible. Where this is not possible, your attorney should make the right decisions on your behalf. The principles are as follows;-

- The presumption of capacity - A person must be assumed to have capacity to make their own decisions, unless it can be established that this is not the case.

- The right to be supported to make a decision - All practical steps must be taken to help a person to make their own decision before anyone concludes that they don't have the capacity to do so.

- The right to make eccentric or unwise decisions - A person should not be treated as unable to make a decision just because they make an unwise decision.

- Best interests - Any decision made or action taken on behalf of people without capacity must be made in their best interests.

- Least restrictive intervention - Anyone making a decision for or on behalf of a person without capacity should consider all effective alternatives and choose the one that is the least restrictive of the person's rights and freedoms.

When someone takes a decision in your best interests they must:

- Do everything possible to encourage you to participate in the decision-making.

- Consider your past and present feelings, taking into account any statement of wishes that you may have made in advance.

- Consider any of your beliefs and values that could influence their decision.

- Consult other people, such as family, carers or friends, who can provide information about your feelings, beliefs and values, and who can help to suggest what might be in your best interests.

Existing Enduring Power of Attorney (EPA)

If you set up an Enduring Power of Attorney (EPA) before 1 October 2007, it might still be valid. You might already be using it without having registered it, so that someone can act on your behalf. This is fine, until you become unable to make your own decisions relating to financial and property matters.

Once this happens, the EPA must be registered before the attorney can take any further action on your behalf. It's the responsibility of your attorney to register the EPA with the Office of the Public Guardian.

Unlike an LPA, an EPA only covers decisions about your property and financial affairs; an attorney doesn't have any power under an EPA to make decisions about your health and welfare. You might want to consider setting up a Personal Welfare LPA to work alongside the existing EPA.

Lacking Capacity to make an LPA or EPA?

If in the future you do not have the mental capacity to make a particular decision, and you have not created a valid LPA or EPA, it may be necessary for the Court of Protection to become involved. The Court of Protection deals with cases relating to the property and welfare of people who may lack capacity. It has the power to:-

- Decide whether someone has the mental capacity to make a decision.

- Make an order relating to the personal welfare or property and financial affairs of someone who lacks mental capacity.

- Appoint a deputy to make decisions on behalf of someone who lacks mental capacity.

Therefore if someone wants to be able to make decisions on your behalf and you have not made an LPA or EPA, they can apply to the court to be appointed as deputy. This is a similar role to that of attorney. The court will consider whether it is necessary for ongoing decisions to be made on your behalf, and whether that person is suitable to be appointed to that role.

Where there is an existing EPA, the attorney may apply to act as a deputy in certain circumstances. However, in some cases, rather than appointing a deputy, the court will make a one-off decision if it is appropriate.

Further information can be obtained from the gov.uk website.

Chapter Fifteen
Trusts - an Overview

THE SUBJECT OF trusts is hugely complex, and this book does not intend to cover very much other than the basics. If you need advice about establishing a trust, or want advice about an existing trust, I strongly recommend you take professional advice.

A trust is a way of managing assets (money, investments, land, buildings etc) for people. There are different types of trusts and they are all taxed differently.

Trusts involve:

- The 'settlor' - the person who puts assets into a trust
- The 'trustee' - the person who manages the trust
- The 'beneficiary' - the person who benefits from the trust.

Trusts may be established for a number of reasons, these include:

- Controlling and protecting family assets
- When someone is too young to handle their affairs
- If someone is unable to manage their affairs because they're incapacitated
- To pass assets on while you're still alive
- To pass assets on when you die (using a 'will trust').

The settlor will decide how the assets in a trust should be used and this is usually detailed in a document called the 'trust deed'.

The trustees are the legal owners of the assets held in a trust. The trustees can change, but there always has to be at least one trustee. Their role is to:

- Deal with the assets according to the trust deed
- Manage the trust on a day-to-day basis and pay any tax due
- Decide how to invest or deploy the trust's assets.

The beneficiaries - and there might be more than one - may benefit from:

- The income of a trust only - for example, rent from a property held in a trust
- The capital only - and becoming the legal owner of the property held in a trust once they reach a certain age
- Both the income and capital of the trust.

Main Types of Trust

Bare trusts - These are where the assets in the trust are held in the name of a trustee but go directly to the beneficiary. The beneficiary has a right to both the capital and income of the trust. Bare trusts are often used to pass assets to young people - the trustees looking after the assets until the beneficiary attains age 18 in England and Wales, or 16 in Scotland.

Interest in possession trusts - These are trusts where the trustee must pass on all trust income to the beneficiary as it arises (less any expenses).

Discretionary trusts - These are where the trustees can decide how to use the trust income, and sometimes the capital. Depending on the trust deed, trustees can decide:

- What is paid out (income and/or capital)
- Which beneficiary will receive payment
- The frequency of payments
- Any other conditions that may be imposed on the beneficiaries.

Discretionary trusts are often established to put assets aside for:

- A future need, for example, a child who may need more financial help than other beneficiaries at some future point in their life.
- Beneficiaries who aren't capable or responsible enough to deal with money themselves.

Accumulation trusts - Where trustees can accumulate income within the trust, and add it to the trust's capital. They may also be able to pay the income out, just as with discretionary trusts.

The tax position of trusts isn't always favourable, and some trusts suffer tax as though they were paying tax at the highest individual rates even on relatively low incomes or capital gains.

Trusts and Income Tax

Different types of trust income are liable to Income Tax at different rates.

For Accumulation or Discretionary trusts the trustees are responsible for paying tax on income received by the trust. The first £1,000 is taxed at the standard rate income tax rate.

Where the settlor has created more than one trust, this £1,000 is divided by the number of trusts they have. However, if the settlor has set up 5 or more trusts, the standard rate band for each trust is £200.

For trust income up to £1,000 tax is paid at 10% for dividends, and 20% for all other income. For annual income above £1,000 the dividend tax rate is 37.5% and all other income is taxed at 45%. There's a 10% tax credit on dividends from UK companies (and some non-UK companies) because the dividends come from profits on which the companies have already paid tax.

For Interest in possession trusts the trustees are responsible for paying Income Tax at a rate of 10% for dividends, and 20% for all other income. Sometimes the trustees will mandate the income direct to the beneficiaries, so that it goes directly to them. If this happens, the beneficiary needs to include this income on their Self Assessment tax return and pay tax on it.

Bare trusts - If you're the beneficiary of a bare trust you're responsible for paying tax on income received from it. You then need to tell HMRC about the income on your Self Assessment tax return.

Other types of trust - There are special tax rules for parental trusts for children, trusts for vulnerable people and trusts set up or managed by people living abroad, called non-resident trusts.

Trusts and Capital Gains Tax

Capital Gains Tax is a tax payable on the profit when you sell, give away, exchange or transfer an asset that has increased in value.

Trusts have an annual tax-free allowance of half the standard capital gains tax allowance available to individuals. If the beneficiary is a disabled person the trust receives the same allowance as an individual person's allowance. The trustees only pay tax if the increase in the value of the asset value is greater than the annual allowance.

For trustees, the Capital Gains Tax rate is 28% - but this could be lower if they qualify for Entrepreneurs' Relief. Trustees calculate their Capital Gains Tax in the same way as everyone else.

Capital Gains Tax is also due when assets are transferred into a trust. In this situation, the person who makes the transfer (the settlor) pays the tax. There's one exception - the settlor can ask for the tax to be postponed (called 'Hold-Over Relief') until the trustees sell or transfer the asset. The trustees may be able to claim further Hold-Over Relief when they sell or transfer the asset.

When assets are transferred away from a trust the trustees pay the tax unless the trust is a bare trust. In this case, if the trustees transfer assets to the beneficiary there's no tax to pay. But if the trustees sell or transfer assets on behalf of the beneficiary, the beneficiary pays.

Trusts and Inheritance Tax

Inheritance Tax may have to be paid on a person's estate when they die. It's due if the estate is worth more than the individual threshold of £325,000 - or £650,000 if they benefit from their deceased spouse's exemption.

Inheritance Tax is due at 40% on anything above the threshold of £325,000 - but there's a reduced rate of 36% if the person's will leaves more than 10% of their estate to charity.

Inheritance Tax may also apply when you're alive if you transfer assets into certain types of trust. In this situation Inheritance Tax is due when assets are transferred into a trust, also when a trust reaches a 10-year anniversary of when it was set up (there are 10-yearly Inheritance Tax charges), and finally when assets are transferred out of a trust ('exit charges') or the trust ends.

Some trusts are treated differently to others for Inheritance Tax purposes.

Bare trusts - Transfers into a bare trust may be exempt from Inheritance Tax, as long as the person making the transfer survives for 7 years after making the transfer.

Interest in possession trusts - These are trusts where the beneficiary is entitled to trust income as it's produced. On assets transferred into this type of trust before 22 March 2006, there's no Inheritance Tax to pay. On assets transferred on or after 22 March 2006, the 10-yearly Inheritance Tax periodic charge may be due.

During the life of the trust there's no Inheritance Tax to pay as long as the asset stays in the trust and remains the 'interest' of the beneficiary. Between 22 March 2006 and 5 October 2008 beneficiaries of an interest in possession trust could pass on their interest in possession to other beneficiaries, for example, to their children. This was called making a 'transitional serial interest' and there's no Inheritance Tax to pay in this situation.

However, from 5 October 2008 beneficiaries of an interest in possession trust can no longer pass their interest on as a transitional serial interest. If an interest is transferred after this date there may be an immediate tax charge of 20% and 10-yearly periodic Inheritance Tax charges may be payable (special rules apply to a vulnerable person trust).

If you inherit an interest in possession trust from someone who has died, there will be no Inheritance Tax at the 10-year anniversary. However, 40% tax will be due when you die.

Trusts for bereaved minors and vulnerable persons have a special tax regime that is too complicated for this book. When contemplating a trust in either of these situations, appropriate specialist advice should be sought, for completeness a very brief overview is provided below:

Trusts for Vulnerable People

Some trusts for disabled people or children will receive special tax treatment. They're called 'trusts for vulnerable beneficiaries'. A vulnerable beneficiary is either:

- Someone who's mentally or physically disabled
- Someone under 18 whose parent has died.

In a trust with a vulnerable beneficiary, the trustees are entitled to a deduction from their Income Tax bill. It's calculated like this:

1. The Trustees calculate what the trust Income Tax charge would be if there was no claim for special treatment - this will vary according to which type of trust it is.

2. They then work out what Income Tax the vulnerable person would have paid if the trust income had been paid directly to them as an individual.

3. They can then claim the difference between these 2 figures as a deduction from their own Income Tax liability.

Capital Gains Tax may also be due if trust assets are sold, given away, exchanged or transferred in another way, and they've gone up in value since being placed into trust.

Tax is only paid by trustees if the assets have increased in value above the 'annual exempt amount', which is an allowance of £10,900 for disabled people (2013/14 tax year) or half that amount, being the standard trust allowance.

Trustees are also responsible for paying any Capital Gains Tax due. If the trust is for vulnerable people, trustees can claim a reduction, which is calculated like this:

1. They work out what they would pay if there was no reduction.

2. They then work out what the beneficiary would have to pay if the gains had come directly to them.

3. They can claim the difference between these two amounts as a reduction on what they have to pay in Capital Gains Tax. This special Capital Gains Tax treatment doesn't apply in the tax year when the beneficiary dies.

Chapter Sixteen
Dealing with Pensions on Death

The State Pension

If your spouse dies and is already receiving a State Pension, their personal representative or family member should inform the Pension Service so that they can stop paying the pension.

If you're the surviving spouse - or civil partner - you may be able to use the deceased's National insurance contribution record to increase your own basic state pension. This will only apply if you're not already entitled to a full State Pension on your own account. Your entitlement depends on whether you've paid National Insurance contributions for at least 30 years.

If you've not yet reached State Pension age you should be able to claim bereavement benefits instead. Then, when reaching retirement age, you can use your spouse's National Insurance record to increase your basic State Pension.

The maximum you will be able to receive is the full basic State Pension. In addition, your spouse or partner might also have been receiving an additional State Pension, or made contributions for one in the future. If this is the case, you could be entitled to some of this income – up to a maximum of 50%.

Personal and Company pensions

If you're dealing with someone's affairs after their death, you should check their paperwork to see if they had any personal or occupational pension schemes. It's also worth contacting the Pensions Tracing Service to see if there are any other pensions you don't know about.

If there are any personal or occupational pensions, see if you can determine what sort of pension it is:-

- Defined Contribution pension (sometimes called a DC scheme) – this is where someone (and if it is a workplace pension, usually their employer contributes too) pays into a personal fund which is later converted into an income at retirement.
- Defined Benefit pension (sometimes called a DB scheme) – this type of pension pays out an income on retirement based on the number of years someone's been in the scheme and on their earnings.

Defined Contribution (DC) Pensions

If the deceased person hadn't started their pension, their estate is entitled to a lump sum up to the value of whatever funds are in the pension. If the deceased was under age 75 this lump sum is tax free, otherwise the scheme administrators will deduct tax at a rate of 55% before handing it over. Alternatively, the fund could be used to provide a pension for a surviving partner and/or children, and income tax would be payable on the income. Contact the pension provider or administrator to get the funds.

Where a tax-free lump sum is payable arrangements may have been made for the payments to go direct into a trust. These trusts are often referred to as Spousal Bypass Trusts. Specialist trust advice should be obtained.

However, if the person who died was already retired and had started taking an income from their DC pension the situation is different. If the income is set up to be paid as an annuity, and you are the spouse or civil partner of the deceased, you should contact the annuity provider to see if you could benefit from a 'survivor's annuity'.

The answer will depend on the type of annuity that was originally purchased. Many annuities are set up to pay a 50% widow's pension, but this isn't necessarily always the case. Contact details for the annuity provider should be on any payment slips from the provider.

If the pension income was paid through what's commonly known as an 'income draw-down' rather than an annuity, and you are the spouse, civil partner, or a dependant child, then you could take a lump sum from the remaining pension pot – subject to a hefty tax charge (normally 55%). Alternatively you could continue to draw an income, paying income tax instead.

Some types of annuity also pay out a lump sum if death occurs within the early years of retirement and again this is paid with tax at 55% deducted.

Defined Benefit (DB) Pensions

If the deceased was paying into, or was a member of a defined benefit pension when they died, then most schemes will pay out a lump sum as a multiple of the deceased's salary. Typically the lump sum will be two or four times their salary. If the deceased was under age 75, this will be tax free, otherwise the scheme administrators will deduct tax at 55% before handing it over.

This sort of pension scheme typically also pays a survivor's pension if you are the spouse, civil partner, or dependant child of the person who died. The amount of pension paid to a widow is usually 50% of the pension payable to the member.

If the deceased was already receiving an income from a DB pension, their dependants will probably be entitled to an ongoing income too. How much depends on the pension scheme rules - though typically it is 50% of the members pension.

Payment of a Serious Ill-Health Lump Sum

- If a member is suffering from serious ill-health then, provided certain conditions are met, the scheme administrator may commute any pension entitlement the member has under the scheme, and then pay the member their entire benefit entitlement as a lump sum.

- This is referred to in pension legislation as a serious ill-health lump sum. Although a serious ill-health lump sum in many cases is obtained from commuting the pension entitlement, the legislation also allows payment to be provided under a term life policy if so desired.

- There are five conditions that all must be met in order for a payment to be treated as a serious ill-health lump sum. These are:-

- Before making the payment the scheme administrator has received written evidence from a registered medical practitioner confirming that the member is expected to live for less than one year.

- The member has not used up all of their pension lifetime allowance at the point the payment is made.

- The payment extinguishes the member's entitlement to benefits under the arrangement (thus all of the benefits under the arrangement must be commuted and paid as a serious ill-health lump sum).

- The payment is made before the member reaches their 75th birthday (there is no minimum age limit on payment of a serious ill-health lump sum).

- The payment is made in respect of what the legislation refers to as an uncrystallised arrangement - i.e. a pension that has not previously paid pension benefits to the member.

Glossary

BENEFICIARY - In the widest sense is a natural person or other legal entity who receives money or other benefits from a benefactor. The beneficiary of a life insurance policy is the person who receives the payment of the sum assured after the death of the insured. The beneficiaries of a trust are the persons with equitable ownership.

CAPACITY - A person's ability to perform a given task such as managing their own finances, or other day-to-day activities. In a legal context it refers to a person's ability to make a decision which has legal consequences.

CAPITAL GAINS TAX (CGT) - the tax that is paid on the realization of profits from selling something for a higher price than it was acquired at.

ENDURING POWER OF ATTORNEY (EPA) - A power of attorney that remains valid even if the person granting it loses mental capacity –EPAs have now been replaced by Lasting Powers of Attorney. See also Power of Attorney.

EQUITABLE OWNERSHIP - Describes the rights of a trust beneficiary in the trust property, as opposed to the legal ownership, which rests in the name of the trustee.

ESTATE - A person's property and possessions, and the total extent of the real and personal property of a deceased person.

EXECUTOR - The person named in a Will who has responsibility for making sure the Will is administered in accordance with the deceased's wishes. It can be a lawyer or it could be a family member or friend.

GRANT OF PROBATE - see probate.

INCOME TAX - the tax that is paid on income received, whether treated as earned income (from employment or a pension), or other forms of income such as rent from a property.

INHERITANCE - something that is or may be inherited; property passing at the owner's death to the heir, or those entitled to succeed.

INHERITANCE TAX - the tax paid by the estate of a deceased person.

INTESTATE - when a person dies without leaving a valid Will.

JOINT TENANCY - joint tenancy is a form of ownership by two or more persons of the same property. The individuals are called joint tenants, and share equal ownership of the property and have the equal, undivided right to keep or dispose of the property. Joint tenancy creates a Right of Survivorship. This right provides that if any one of the joint tenants dies, the remainder of the property is transferred to the survivors.

LAST WILL AND TESTAMENT - The legal document that specifies a person's final wishes, as pertaining to his/her possessions and dependents. A person's last will and testament will outline what to do with possessions, and what will happen to other things for which they are responsible, such as custody of dependants.

LASTING POWER OF ATTORNEY LPA - a power of attorney that remains valid even if the person granting it loses mental capacity.

LETTER OF ADMINISTRATION - the Scottish equivalent of a grant of probate.

OCCUPATIONAL PENSION - A pension scheme, established by an employer for its employees, and is a form of deferred remuneration. The pension income is paid on the retirement of the individual member.

POWER OF ATTORNEY - This is a legal document that authorises one or more people to handle someone else's affairs. This can be for an indefinite period, for a limited amount of time, or to deal with a specific situation.

PRIVATE PENSION - Known as a Personal Pension, and is a pension arrangement set up by individuals whether they are in employment or self-employment. It has similar rules and tax treatment to an Occupational Pension scheme.

PROBATE - The legal process of administering someone's estate when they have died.

SETTLOR - The person who settles property on trust law for the benefit of beneficiaries.

SPOUSAL BYPASS TRUST - the name given to a trust arrangement that seeks to mitigate inheritance tax by placing into trust, assets that would otherwise be paid direct to a spouse. Thus potentially bypassing the spouse and on their death, passing to other beneficiaries.

TENANTS IN COMMON - All tenants in common hold an individual, undivided ownership interest in the property. This means that each party has the right to alienate, or transfer the ownership of, his/her ownership interest. This can be done by deed, will, or other legal conveyance.

TRUST - A legal arrangement in which a person (the Trustee) holds property (this can be land or money) of another (the Settlor) for the benefit of a third party (the beneficiary).

WILL - See Last Will and Testament.

Suggested Reading

I'M AN AVID reader, and can get through several books each a month, on a variety of subjects. In the context of death, grief, money and happiness several books stand out which I share here. It's impossible to list all the books I want to recommend, but for a wider list of recommended books please visit www.yellowtail.co.uk/book-reviews/

A Widow's Story: A memoir by Joyce Carol Oates

"My husband died, my life collapsed" writes the author on the loss of her husband of 48 years. She had driven him to hospital where he was diagnosed with pneumonia, a week later he was dead. She describes the initial stages of grief, and her bewilderment following his death. It is a very introspective account of loss, grief and bereavement.

An experienced writer she ably describes how her world totally changes with his death. She describes her isolation which is instant and relentless. This book has been described by other widows as a perfect account of the after death emotional roller coaster.

The Year of Magical Thinking - Joan Didion

Like Joyce Carol Oates, Joan Didion is an accomplished writer who gives an unflinching account of the sudden loss of her husband following cardiac arrest (his death occurred while their only child was in a coma in a hospital). It is an honest, but not overly sentimental account - some readers have described her a cool - perhaps because she doesn't offer vague platitudes or advice.

She simply relates her very personal experience. She describes her inevitable vulnerability and the unexpected moments of being engulfed by memories and sudden tears. It is a different book to Oates' though both women are of a similar age, are both writers, and know each other.

A Widow's Story - Anita Gatehouse

Anita is a financial planner, and we have known each other for several years having met on one of Dr Maria Nemeth's 'Mastering Life's Energies' coaching courses. We both have experience advising widows, and Anita has written a book outlining the steps to be taken by the recently bereaved widow who must now take responsibility for her financial decisions.

It has the potential to be an overwhelming subject, but Anita approaches it by asking her readers to take things one step at a time. It is a straightforward, no nonsense text that will lead the widow toward making better financial decisions.

The D-Word: Talking about Dying: A Guide for Relatives, Friends and Carers - Sue Brayne

The premise of my book is that people don't talk about death, and they don't talk about the impact of death on their financial situation. The D Word, provides a sound basis for starting these conversations, particularly for people where death may be imminent. Talking about Dying is a difficult discussion to begin, but is very necessary. Sue's approach is gentle and helpful.

The Number - Lee Eisenberg

If death is a taboo subject, money is not far behind. The Number was the first book I read where I felt compelled to buy a copy for each of my clients. It describes in ordinary language the idea that we each have a 'number' to aim for. The number being the amount of money we need to accumulate so as to be able to enjoy a desired quality of life to the very end. In 2007 I gave away 100 copies and even now, several years later, clients still tell me how useful it was. It demystifies what financial planning is all about.

Mastering Life's Energies - Dr Maria Nemeth

Maria has become a friend and a mentor to me, and my family. I heard about her work several years ago and then attended a week long course called 'Mastering Life's Energies'. I have subsequently returned to discover more of Maria's work and to develop my coaching skills.

This book recognises that whilst we all have rare moments of luminosity, we tend to approach life stuck in old habits and routines. To live the lives we truly yearn for requires us to ditch our old ways, and develop new habits, strategies and ways of thinking. Easier said than done, but Maria guides the reader though their doubts and fears so that they can make those changes.

Happy Money - Elizabeth Dunn & Michael Norton

The premise of this book is that to be happy, we need to use our money differently. Most of us use money to provide short-term rewards to compensate for our hard work and often less than satisfactory lives. But this approach is wrong according to the authors, and they cite the most recent psychological studies to support this.

There are, they say, five ways to use money that will lead to greater happiness, and they go through each of the five ways in detail. The book confirms most of what I have already come to understand about money and happiness, but puts it across in an easy manner.

About the Author

DENNIS HALL IS the founder of Yellowtail Financial Planning, a firm of independent financial advisers located in Central London. He has been advising private clients for more than twenty-five years following an earlier career in the Royal Marines.

He is an award winning Chartered Financial Planner, an Associate of the Personal Finance Society and the Institute of Financial Planning, and a Member of the Chartered Securities Institute. In the past he has been the FT's Money Management; Retirement Planner of the Year and Investment Company Planner of the Year, and runner up Inheritance Tax Planner of the Year. He has also been voted the unbiased.co.uk Media IFA of the Year, and is a CityWire Top 100 Financial Planner.

He lives in Central London with his wife Akiko, and outside financial planning his interests include cooking, fine wine, movies and contemporary art. He likes to pursue one new challenge each year and in the past this has included completing the Marathon de Sables, cycling from Lands End to John O'Groats, and most recently, doing Stand Up comedy.